THE SONG
OF THE PLOW

By EDMUND GOSSE, C.B., LL.D.
COLLECTED POEMS. Fcap. 8vo, 5s. net.

By LAURENCE HOPE.
Demy 8vo, 5s. net each.
THE GARDEN OF KAMA.
INDIAN LOVE.
STARS OF THE DESERT.

By FIONA MACLEOD.
COLLECTED WORKS. 7 vols. Crown 8vo,
5s. net each.
   I. PHARAIS: THE MOUNTAIN LOVERS.
  II. THE SIN EATER: THE WASHER OF THE
      FORD.
 III. THE DOMINION OF DREAMS: UNDER
      THE DARK STAR.
 IV. THE DIVINE ADVENTURER: IONA:
      STUDIES IN SPIRITUAL HISTORY.
  V. THE WINGED DESTINY: STUDIES IN THE
      SPIRITUAL HISTORY OF THE GAEL.
 VI. THE SILENCE OF AMOR: WHERE THE
      FOREST MURMURS.
VII. POEMS AND DRAMAS.

By JOHN MASEFIELD.
Crown 8vo. 3s. 6d. net each.
DAUBER.
THE DAFFODIL FIELDS.
PHILIP THE KING.
THE FAITHFUL. (A PLAY)

By SAROJINI NAIDU.
POEMS OF LIFE AND DEATH. 5s. net.
THE BIRD OF TIME. 5s. net.
THE GOLDEN THRESHOLD. 3s. 6d.

By WILLIAM SHARP.
(FIONA MACLEOD.)
SELECTED WRITINGS. 5 vols. Crown 8vo.
5s. net each.
   I. POEMS.
  II. STUDIES AND APPRECIATIONS.
 III. PAPERS CRITICAL AND REMINISCENT.
 IV. LITERARY GEOGRAPHY AND TRAVEL
      SKETCHES.
  V. VISTAS. THE GIPSY CHRIST AND OTHER
      PROSE IMAGININGS.

By ARTHUR SYMONS.
POEMS. 2 vols. Demy 8vo. 10s. net.
KNAVE OF HEARTS. Demy 8vo. 5s. net.
TRAGEDIES. Demy 8vo. 5s. net.

LONDON: WILLIAM HEINEMANN.

THE SONG OF THE PLOW: 🌿 🌿 🌿 🌿 🌿

BEING THE ENGLISH CHRONICLE

BY MAURICE HEWLETT

LONDON: WILLIAM HEINEMANN

🌿 🌿 🌿 🌿 🌿 🌿 🌿 🌿

First published October 1916.
New Edition November 1916.

London : William Heinemann, 1916.

The Dedication to England, long divided, now made one

HERE'S of your children, O Mother dear,
　　Here's of your dead, our brothers and
　　　sons ;
Norman and English, they lie there
Facing in death the tyrant's guns ;
　　English marrow and Norman blood　　　　5
　　Welded against the horded Huns.
One house, one hope, one brotherhood,
　　Patient hand clasping hand of pride,
　　Fronting one barrier to the flood ;
And happy so if they have died　　　　　　10
　　Saining with life-blood that old wound,
　　Stopping that gaping rent and wide
'Twixt men and masters of the ground,
　　That old unquencht unending strife
　　'Twixt serf and despot, free and bond.　　15
Ev'n as a man by his dead wife,

DEDICATION TO ENGLAND

Stabbed by his loneliness and pain,
  Will stroke the handle of the knife
Whose reddened steel makes his love plain,
  And read in every bitter pang   20
  Witness of her, and own a gain,
In smarting tear and salt blood-tang
  That speak to him of his dear dead—
  So, England, when the trumpets rang
And young men stream'd to face the dread   25
  Of rocking battle, anguish wove
  A mist of glory for my head,
Seeing you transfigured, and our love
  A living spirit, and our men
  One kindred ! Here is stuff enough   30
Of victory to fire the pen
  Of him who saw your ravaged heart
  Laid bare to scorn, and loved you then
As never yet ; and felt tears start
  Which, gushing up from hidden springs   35
  Deeply within his inmost part,
Floated him high o'er mortal things,
  To see from evil lift the good,
  And wait the flickering of the wings
Of man immortally renewed,   40
  Lord of a rid and garnisht earth,
  Swept with a besom dipt in blood !

PREFACE

THIS poem, which a sense of decorum, but not common sense, forbade me to call *The Hodgiad*, was conceived some ten years ago, at a time, that is, when I was closely in touch with the hero of it. I have been at work upon it or concerned about it ever since. Its subject is as old as England, but the point of view, I think, is novel; therefore I offer a few words of explanation of its scope. It will be seen by any one who chooses to reflect upon it that this country holds two classes of persons, a governing class, and a governed class. Herein it does not differ perhaps from a good many other undemocratic states; but it differs remarkably in this, that with us the governing and the governed classes are two separate nations. By race the governed are British with a strong English mixture of blood; the governing class is by race even now preponderatingly Latin-French with a Scandinavian admixture : by tradition, breeding, and education it is entirely so. All the apparatus, all the science, all the circumstance of government are still Norman. It may be that the governed race has been granted, between 1832 and 1883, an increasing share in government. It has been granted it, but has not taken it up. Now, speaking generally, this *Song of the Plow* is a history of the governed race from the date of the Norman Conquest, that successful raid made a conquest by the acquiescence of the raided, when foreigners acquired an ascendancy which they have never yet dropped. Not only so, but they have never yet ceased to be foreign to the race which they rule. The tale, in its parts, may be the stuff for prose ; in its broad outlines, in its masses of lights and darks, it is a highly poetical subject. In its process of obstinate, fluctuating conflict between privilege and custom, between instinct to rule and instinct to be free, it is an epic subject, perhaps the only real one left. To put it in Aristotle's manner, when he hit off *The Odyssey* in three lines—

The Argument

A certain man, being in bondage to a proud Conqueror, maintained his customs, nourisht his virtues, obeyed his tyrants, and at the end of a thousand years found himself worse off than he was in the beginning of his servitude. He then lifted his head, lookt his master in the face, and his chains fell off him.

That is succinctly the Argument of this Poem.

PREFACE

Those words were written in 1913, before
the horror and menace of German despotry were
guessed by the world of men. As for the War,
and our part in it, it is yet too early to do more
than dream what the upshot for humanity may
be ; but of some things done, already historical,
I have written in the Envoy to this poem, and
other things, which my heart bids me hope for,
I have prefigured. Nothing in history had
prepared us for the uprising of our Peasantry so
soon as the issue was plain : it was wonderful
that they rose, still more wonderful that they
should have seen what was really at stake. By
those two acts they declared themselves at once
responsible citizens and the equals of their
masters. My hope is that their masters may
not forget, since they themselves certainly will
not. If a war which has stultified the very
Idea of Manhood has nevertheless made the
British and their governors one people, it is
worth the horror and the shame; and our sons'
sons may bless the Germans unawares.

CONTENTS

PRELUDE

THE MAN ON THE HILL

THE MAN ON THE HILL

ain and
he Plow.

I SING the Man, I sing the Plow
 Ten centuries at work, and Thee,
 England, whom men with pence enow
Profanely call Home of the Free.
 Enslav'd, back-broken, driv'n afield,   5
 Ask him I sing how this may be,
Him that the slipping share must wield,
 And wring his brow that others eat,
 And see them fatten on his yield,
And by his pain derive their meat :   10
 Hodge, hireling for a thousand years,
 To whom the burden and the heat
To reap in sweat the sown in tears
 Must be, whatever else betide ;
 Pinned to his rood thro' hopes and fears 15
Till they he served, unsatisfied
 With having all but that, took care
 To get that too—Hodge crucified,
Like Him Who on His rood hung bare !
 Of those his muted æons of pain,   20
 Dumb child of suffering and to spare,

THE SONG OF THE PLOW

I sing the grumbled low refrain,
   The broken heartstrings' undertones
   Which thro' the clash and gallant strain
Of warring legions, thro' the groans   25
   Of them they war on, thro' the blent
   Organs and trumpets, creaks and drones
The lordings' way to tournament,
   To love of women, pride of men,
   To crowning or to parliament.   30
Here's homespun for your handselling then,
   You who have fingers for such thrums :
   Let the dark angel teach my pen
The underchant which all the drums
   That go before to cry our lord   35
   Can never stifle, that which comes
A bourdon from the tilth and sward,
   Not to be quencht, outshrilled in vain
   By clarion trumpet or bare sword—
Nay, but like constancy of rain,   40
   Heard thro' the thunder of the guns
   Adown the hillside, o'er the plain,
Across the river. Ah, patient ones,
   They heard it then, they know it now ;
   Say, shall it speak in vain their sons,   45
The creaking of thy driven plow ?
   O to whom all my song must be
   If it would thrive, receive it Thou,
This epic of an agony !

4

The
Pro-
agonist.

The shepherd upon a hill he sat,   50
He had his tabard and his hat,
His tarbox, his pipe and flagat,
And his name was called Jolly Wat;
For he was a good herd's boy, Ut hoy!
For in his pipe he made such joy.   55

Under the sun on the gray hill,
  At breakfast campt behind the hedge,
There ate he, there eats he still
Bread and bacon on the knife's edge.
  Blow the wind chill, be sky of lead,   60
  Or let the sun burn o'er the ridge,
Or be the cloudy fleeces spread,
  Or let rain drive, or snow come dry
  What time the blackthorn flower is shed
Like puffs of smoke on the blue sky—   65
  There sits he now as he sat then
  And watches how the year goes by,
And sees the world God made for men
  As little for them as it was
  In those old days of Cæsar's when   70
Lord Christ came riding on an ass,
  Borrowed from out some friendly stall,
  Or lifted from the common grass
And set to this new festival.
  So then to work, with heavy foot,   75
  To rouse his horses with a call;

5

And slow as they he puts them to 't,
  To hail the plow on the stony down
  Thro' marl and flint, thro' stock and root,
Where the rooks cloud the strip of brown   80
  And querulous peewits wheel and flock :
  Behold them on the sky-line thrown
Like giant shapes of riven rock,
  He and his team on the world's rim
  Creeping like the hands of a clock.   85
Or in wet meadows plashy and dim
  When winter winds blow shrill and keen,
  See him bank up the warp and swim
The eddying water over the green ;
  Or follow up the hill the sheep   90
  To where the kestrels soar and lean,
And from her form the hare doth leap
  Quick and short, and lightly flies
  Before him up the grassy steep
Where cloakt and crookt he climbs. His eyes, 95
  Seeing all things, and seeking none,
  Are very patient and weather-wise.
The clearest eyesight under the sun
  He has, and holds the ancient way,
  The way his forefathers have gone,   100
And deems himself as wise as they.

The Day's Round.   Afield at five, nuncheon at nine
                      Under the hedge, and at mid-day

Under the hedge to sit and dine ;
  And then to work until the hour   105
  Bid him to slacken hand and line,
Crying him from the gray church tower
  As it hath cried for a thousand year,
  Once for Mary, of maids the flower,
And now for tea and homely cheer.   110
  So down the borstal, into the road,
  Home with beasts and jingling gear,
By park of lord and house of God,
  Betwixt the hedgerows, by the farm,
  By flowering garth, afoot and aplod   115
By the white cottages thatcht and warm,
  To home of wife and child comes he,
  Bent in back and weary of arm,
To such good rest as his may be.
  And so week out till Sunday come,   120
  And then to church and reverie ;
And tho' they preach the gods of Rome,
  And tho' great Christopher still bestride
  The flooded ford, and thro' the gloom
The Lord upon his shoulder ride   125
  In likeness of a young child lost ;
  And tho' mass-music sob and chide
Of God within the blameless Host,
  And far-off twinkling candles name
  The presence of the Holy Ghost—   130
His homely God is still the same,

With earth-clots clinging to his flanks :
  A God of cloud instead of flame,
A God for wonder, not for thanks ;
  A shrouded bulk inscrutable, 135
  Who chooses few and slays by ranks
The toilers ; who makes corn to swell
  Or bids it wither in the blade ;
  Who bides his time and will not tell
Whether a man should be afraid 140
  To slake his need, or bold to slake
  That which he hath with what is laid
Before him, woman, beer, or cake
  Of currant bread upon a platter.
  So Hodge like all of us will make 145
In his own image God, half satyr
  And half an old man masterful—
  As in the old days, so in the latter,
Despite pulpit and Sunday school.
  Thereafter work for fork and knife, 150
  A time to get one's belly full,
And sleep for him beside his wife
  In simple easeful fellowship—
  A sleep, a dream, the law of life
That draws man's lip to woman's lip. 155
  For thus it is that we are gotten
  And mouths are made for bite and sip,
And scion struck ere stock be rotten.
  And so the day is gone with speed,

Hodge at his ease, good fish well shotten,   160
A holy day for the holy deed.

Year's
Round.
    This is the year's round he must go
To make and then to win the seed :
In winter to sow and in March to hoe,
    Michaelmas plowing, Epiphany sheep ;   165
    Come June there is the grass to mow,
At Lammas all the vill must reap.
    From dawn to dusk, from Easter to Lent
    Here are the laws that he must keep :
Out and home goes he, back-bent,   170
    Heavy, patient, slow, as of old
    Father, granfer, ancestor went
O'er Sussex weald and Yorkshire wold.

The
Outlook.
    O what see you from your gray hill ?
    The sun is low, the air all gold,   175
Warm lies the slumbrous land and still.
    I see the river with deep and shallow,
    I see the ford, I hear the mill ;
I see the cattle upon the fallow ;
    And there the manor half in trees,   180
    And there the church and the acre hallow
Where lie your dead in their feretories
    Of clay and dust and crumble of peat,
    With a stone or two to their memories :
Your dead who with their sweat kept sweet   185

This heritage of gray and green,
This England now the richer for it.
I see the yews and the thatch between,
   The smoke that tells of cottage and hearth,
   And all as it has ever been   190
From the beginning on this old earth.
   And so it is even as it was
   From the beginning in Hodge's garth,
While kings and statesmen flaunt and pass,
   Kings and lords and knights of the shire,   195
   Bishops in lawn (rare flesh to be grass !),
Priest and schoolman, clerk and esquire ;
   Danes and Normans and Scottishmen,
   Frenchmen, Brunswickers, son after sire,   199
They come and conquer, they ruffle and reign,
   They rule, they ride, they spend, they grudge,
   They bicker their threescore years and ten,
They slay, and thieve, and go ; but Hodge
   The Englishman stoops to fork and flail,
Saint Use.   And serves Saint Use, and will not budge, 205
But drives the furrow and fills the pail,
   Raining sweat lest the land go dry :
   He sees his masters, he gives them hail
With hand to forelock as they ride by—
   They that eat what he doth bake,   210
   They that hold what he must buy,
They that spend what he doth make,
   They that are rich by other men's toil ;

10

THE MAN ON THE HILL

They of the sword and he of the rake,
The lords of the land, the son of the soil !   215
O Christ, the Patron of the Poor,
Thou Who didst suffer harlot's oil
Anoint Thy feet, O narrow Door !
Thou Who didst sanctify our dearth
With bitter pain and anguish sore,   220
A barefoot King held nothing worth—
Here's misery for Thy chrism to mend :
A thousand years to plow the earth,
And be worse off at journey's end !

Question. Thou mute and patient sojourner   225
(So let us ask him, being his friend),
From what dim nation, by what spur
Cam'st thou to serve this long duress ?
Whence came your fathers, hoping here
To win the land and to possess,   230
And gained you for your broad domain
A hireling's hire and wretchedness
After ten centuries of pain ?

Pedigree. " No man can tell how old my stock.
My sires were here before the grain ;   235
They reared that temple of gray rock
Which in a hollow of the hills
Seemeth our constancy to mock,
So little hurt crude usage skills

11

To it, so much to mortal men.   240
They shap't the mist-pool where distils
The blessèd dew ; they died and then
They served their dead with barrow and mound.
With wattled burghs on dun and pen
They made this Albion holy ground,   245
Naming the mountains, pen and dun,
Naming the waters.   First, they found
The lovely service of the sun.
Then bowed their backs to Roman goads
From sea to sea the Wall to run ;   250
The furrows of the long white roads
Are of their driven husbandry :
We bruise their dust still with our loads.
Then came the English oversea,
Of onset wilder than was Rome's,   255
And slew or made our men unfree,
But led our women to their homes
To serve their needs of board and bed,
And get them theows—and so it comes
That I am sprung unwarranted   260
By priest or book or marriage-line ;
Yet south and north my folk are spread
From Thames' mouth to the wells of Tyne.
They moil aland like busy ants
With pick and pack, and make no sign,   265
To sow and garner for the wants
Of man and beast.   This is their hire,

THE MAN ON THE HILL

To cling about their ancient haunts
Tho' son be poorer than his sire.
    Now therefore you shall understand   270
    My folk yet people every shire
From Lizard to Northumberland.
    They till the levels of the east,
    Where blown grass borders the sea-strand,
And in the dunes for man and beast   275
    They win their fodder.   They make fat
    The lean, themselves they profit least;
But this is not to wonder at.
    Where Ouse and Trent and Humber coil
    'Twixt reedy marsh and meadow-flat,   280
Where Thames grows turbid with the moil
    Of London's pool and London's mart,
    They bank the water into soil,
And spread the dung and lead the cart.
    Find you them in the stormy west   285
    Where from long Cleator to the Start
The land meets ocean, crest with crest,
    Throwing her rocky bastions up :
    There is my kindred's upland nest
Who lead their sheep for bite and sup   290
    By mountain path and waterfall
    To where the grass grows in a cup
Of rearing cliff and craggy wall.
    And thence the upland rivers race
    A nobler course ; thence best of all   295

13

Flings Severn down, to earn her grace
   There where she broadens to the main
   And giveth Bristol pride of place.
Go seek my kith on hill and plain,
   Whether in Cumberland's deep dales,   300
   In York's dark moors or Lincoln's fen,
In Westmorland's hill-shadowed vales ;
   From the scarred Peak and splintry Edge,
   By Salop's stony march with Wales,
To grassy boss and grassy ledge,   305
   To pastoral Wilts, to Somerset,
   To Dartmoor holding up her ridge
Against the west wind and the wet ;
   In billowy breadths of open down
   Where the bright rivers ripple and fret,   310
And each hill wears a beechen crown,
   And every village hides in trees ;
   And on the heath, by market town,
By holt and brake, from Axe to Tees—
   Seek there, for there my root is thrown   315
   Between the Eastern and Western seas.
And whence my masters, whence their own,
   And wherefore over us they lord it
   Who are of England's marrow and bone,
The Use is so and doth award it.   320
   To them the land, to us the plow ;
   They take the fruits when we have scored it;
But I eat bread in the sweat of my brow

And hold my wife against my side,
And love her when the lights are low,   325
And call her mine, and bid her bide
  The better or worse of tricksome years,
  As she promised when she was bride.
And so I, Hodge, make shift with my peers."

Quousque tandem ? Is it not his yet, this dear soil,   330
  Rich with his blood and sweat and tears ?
Warm with his love, quick with his toil,
  Where kings and their stewards come and go,
  And take his earnings as tribute royal,
And suffer him keep a shilling or so ?   335
  They come, they pass, their names grow dim;
  He bends to plow, or plies his hoe ;
And what are they to the land or him ?
  They shall perish but he endure
  (Thus saith the Scripture old and grim),   340
He shall shed them like a vesture ;
  But he is the same, his tale untold ;
  And to his sons' sons shall inure
The land whereon he was bought and sold.

BOOK I

THE STAR OF SENLAC

C

BOOK I : THE STAR OF SENLAC

The way is long and very dark
I have to go : be Thou my guide.
Behold, I bring as to an Ark
In waste of waters this to Thy side.
Hold it a moment in Thy hand,
And give me courage and right pride.

hree
ings in
ngland,
)66.

T HERE was a year, I understand,
    A thousand odd since Christ was King,
    There reignèd three kings in England
Ere Christmas bells were due to ring ;
    And after them came never a one   5
    Of English blood for song to sing :
Edward, and Harold Godwinsson,
    And the Bastard of Normandy—
Him they called the Base-begun,
Tho' none the worse for that fared he.   10
    And in that time of high unrest
    Among the high who deem them free,
Hodge the plowman, ridging the crest
    Under the stars with his oxen-team,
Saw the bearded star in the west   15

And markt his mantle of litten steam
   That flew as he flew and foreboded
   Murrain or dearth, and made men dream
O' nights, and women who workt full-loaded
   Drave to bed before their day,   20
   To bring forth children cripple-bodied,
Hare-lipt, riven, halt or splay.
   The summer-tide was slumbrous and hot
   That set in with that Star of May ;
There was no spring feed to be got ;   25
   The corn grew short, there was no air ;
   The land panted ; a man fell shot
By unseen shaft from none knew where,
   Out in the open among his friends,
   Out in the acres parcht and bare.   30
God, He knew to what dreadful ends
   Such wild doings were let to be ;
   But good Saint Michael made amends
When a wet wind blew up from the sea,
   And brought the soak to thirsty lands,   35
   And drave men out to fallow and lea.
So to the plowing went all hands ;
   And what reckt Hodge of Harold the King,
   Of Dives-on-Sea, or Pevensey sands,
Of Norman or of Etheling   40
   Beside the wet for the land's drouth ?
   What of marching and countermarching,
Hotfoot to North, hotfoot to South,

Hob and Lob gone out with the reeve
To sweat and grunt in battle's mouth— 45
Hob and Lob with the fyrd to cleave
e Hoar
ple-
:. To the tryst of the Hoar Apple-tree?
His plow was not for a take-or-leave,
His beast must eat, to work must he
 On the dim cliffs above the shore, 50
 Upon the hills above the sea,
Where rain-fog lulled the shingle's roar
 To a prattle of little ripples awash,
 And sights and sounds were sudden and o'er—
Here for a flash, gone in a flash, 55
 Like sea-birds drifting, like snow that floats,
 A moment lying, then on the brash
Melted—the mist played eyes and throats
 Phantasmagoria with the world,
 What time at sea the fleet of boats 60
Crept north; and ere the Dragon unfurl'd
 To shame the rebels of the north
 The Dragon's lord was southward hurl'd
To meet his dread, and try his worth
 With one who feared no mortal thing 65
 But his own need. That drove him forth—
Immortal hunger: that was king.

aint
`alixtus
ay,
066. On thro' the mist those robbers came
 While Hodge was at his clod-breaking;
For when to gild Saint Calixt's name 70

21

Uprose the autumnal sun that day
And the earth reekt beneath his flame,
Hodge fared to work ; he might not stay,
  Tho' hill wagged head to hill, or leapt
  The tall elm-trees like storks at play ;   75
He must abroad while the beasts slept
  (Altho' the Kings of the earth stood up)
  To win them fodder. His way he crept
While Normans take the Blessèd Sop ;
  While his kindred mutter and snore   80
  And daylight brimmeth the sky's cup,
He takes the road, he leads the store
  To pasture, or yokes-to his cattle,
  And drives his furrow a lugg or more
While trumpets shatter and drums rattle,   85
  And kings and the herds they drive take breath
  For plunge in the red bath of battle.

The Dance of Death. What's to him this Dance of Death,
  Or this young man that jigs for his lord,
  Young Taillefer, as the tale saith,   90
Flaunting or tossing up his sword,
  Singing of Charlemagne and the Peers
  To dare the Englishman and his horde ?
What's it to him how the flood veers,
  Spilling on Senlac's bare ledge ?   95
  'Tis nine by the sun, as it appears,
Time for nuncheon under the hedge.

Loose your kerchief of bread and porret,
Sit you down and cut you a wedge,
And chew deep-breathing, the better for it ;   100
Nor any the worse for the murder-bout
Five mile hence, as a bird would score it—
Murder, havoc, hatred and rout,
Foul blood-letting that makes men beasts;
English grunting their harsh *Out ! Out !*   105
And shaven Normans, smooth as priests,
Countergrunting their *Dex nous aide !*
Or how the onset creeps and twists
Round and about thro' the hazel-glade
And up the slope to th' embattled brood   110
Of Godwin's sons in shield-stockade !
Hodge is amunch while the mailèd flood
Of hungry thieves and rascalry
Slays and sacks the chiefs of his blood,
And gets again to his husbandry,   115
And drives his plow till the tardy sun
Goes down bloody into the sea ;
And homeward then, the day's work done—
Calixtus' day, when a king was shot,
And a new king trod him, a wench's son.   120

The Bastard and his men. O lord of a realm, or a three-perch plot,
What will you do with your pair of hands
But hold your fistful ?   Your headpiece hot
May rule that which it understands :

23

The rest is vanity.   What gained   125
  The Bastard by his doubled lands ?
He sweated double who twice reigned.
  But Hodge, who changed his burly lord,
  The sleepy, easy, beery-veined,
For hatchety Norman, tense as a cord—   130
  Curt-voiced Héricourt, Grantmesnil,
  Tibetot, Botetort, Ralf Flambard,
Perci, d'Albini, Mandeville,
  D'Eu, d'Avranches, Lacy or Verdun—
  He changed his master but not his vill ;   135
He called old Stoke a new Stoke-Farden,
  And drave his plow in the old furrow :
  The land he knows bears a new burden,
The same good sun will shine to-morrow ;
  Tho' Ralf be reeve in place of Grim,   140
  The new manor is the old boro',
And all is one to the likes of him,
  So he may earn his bent back's worth.
  He savours October rich and dim,
The sweet sharp smell of the wet earth ;   145
  The dying fall, the woodland sere,
  The taint of death that is promise of birth,
A glory of gold for the world's bier
  (O dewy hillside ! O tall tree !) :
  Thanks giveth he for the fading year.   150
Such good content, good Lord, give me !

THE STAR OF SENLAC

Hodge and his land.

Hodge hath his plot of land, to love it
  (If he is bond, his love is free);
Though Gurth may have a full half-bovate
  Of deep land in the Blackacre,   155
  And book behind him which will prove it,
And pasture for his pence a year ;
  While Hodge have nought but his poor pightle,
  Lifted by moonlight here or there,
Held God knows how, by no writ title,   160
  The root's in him by saw which says,
  What's done is done without requital ;
To-morrows shall be as yesterdays ;
  And so for ever ! Saints enough
  Has Holy Church for priests to praise ;   165
But the chief of saints for workday stuff
  Afield or at board is good Saint Use,
  Withal his service is rank and rough ;
Nor hath he altar nor altar-dues,
  Nor boy with bell, nor psalmodies,   170
  Nor folk on benches, nor family pews—
Yet he is Hodge's and Hodge his,
  And holding to him these days of dread,
  Hodge the bondman may work at ease
And munch at ease his leek and bread,   175
  Let rime or flower be on the thorn,
  And English Harold alive or dead.
But he must bend to his lord's corn
  (Follow him thro' returning moons !) ;

THE SONG OF THE PLOW

*Boone-
work.*

From the wet winter when wheat is born 180
Every season hath its Boones—
Sowing, harrowing, reaping, carrying
Thro' dripping or thro' burning noons.
He guards the blade against bird-harrying,
He hoes, and then with sickle and stick 185
Harvests, with the girl he's marrying
Hard at his heels ; and so to the rick,
And so to fork and flail and van
Go man and woman, hearty or sick,
Hodge with his wife, maid with her man— 190
John Stot's daughter, the brown-eyed lass
With ripening breast and neck of tan,
Fifteen year old come Candlemass.
Unfree, unfree, bound to his vill,
Plodding his rounds like blinkered ass 195
That draws the well ; at his lord's will,

Bondage.

There where he sweats there he must bide ;
No Jack of him may have his Jill
Unless he buy her to his side ;
No Jack may win the monk's fair crown, 200
Nor make the Body of Him Who died
That men might live. That Head hung down
For gentlemen, as it would seem,
Unless some day Christ know His own.

*William
is King.*

Dead is King Harold, sped his dream ; 205
They choose the Bastard, crown his sword.

26

He's burnt the North, by Avon's stream
He's called the West to know him lord.
  A lord he is, who rules with might
  The welter of his brigand horde :   210
No man dare trespass in his sight
  Which oversees from Tweed to Seine ;
  No man dare question his good right
From Cheviot to the march of Maine.
  Stark lord, the emblems of whose power 215
  This beaten realm doth yet retain
In Lincoln's castle, London's tower,
  On Durham's eyrie river-girt,
  And where Ely abode the hour
Of Cromwell's rod and Hitch's hurt.   220
  So up and down and back and forth
  The strong king goes with spears alert ;
He cows the West, he hounds the North,
  Till all this realm is in his grip.
  Now he will reckon his work's worth. 225

Sarum,
1086.   The empty leagues where Sarum's keep,
  Islanded lonely in the grass,
  Watches the shepherd and the sheep
Behold him now. Before him pass
  His bailiffs and commissioners 230
  To tell the acres each man has
In fee from him. He sits, he hears,
  Huge crimsoned bulk of little ease ;

But never a tittle slips his ears,
And never baron 'scapes his knees   235
   Whereat to kneel and touch his hands
   And do him homage and fealties,
With suit and service for his lands.

Domesday. And every due of every wight
   Within this England written stands   240
For all to read who have the sight :
   Sokemen so many, tenants-at-will,
   Cotsetters, men of tenant right;
The kine, the pigs, the weirs, the mill;
   Villeins with their oxen and plows—   245
   There wrought no man in any vill
But he was reckoned with his house.
   And as in good Saint Edward's days
   So must it go, Saint Use allows,
When Norman lords ride English ways.   250
   Just was this king, and cared not flinch
   To give or take, to ruin or raise.
He took his ell and spared his inch—
   That was his freedom as he viewed it;
   By hook or crook he got the kinch   255
Upon his rascals, or they rued it
   At rope's end.   So with humour grim
   And harsh he sought peace and ensued it,
And died; and peace held after him.
   And after him to this our day   260
The Nor- The Norman and his Sanhedrim
man hold.
28

Have held the land in triple sway—
  By sword, by use, by lawmaking;
  And yet more Norman even than they
Is he who climbs within the ring   265
  Of Privilege and learns the rite
  Which Normans had from their dead king.
" I am thy man," so sware his knight,
  " In life and limb, and will keep faith
  With thee and thine in wrong or right   270
From this time forth thro' life and death."
  God knows they have not shunned to die,
  And wear their honour like a wreath;
And no man knows it more than I.
  Yet mark: while lords by Sarum's hold   275
  Debated how estates should lie
'Twixt suzerain and mesne, burnt gold
  Was on the wheat, and Hodge afield
  Laid-to the sickle.   So of old
Shepherds were watching on the weald   280
  While kings and sages came athrong
  To seek the new-born Lord, revealed
Withal in starry outpoured song
  To those poor humble-minded clowns
  Keeping their flocks there all night long.   285

Rufus, Dead or alive, King William frowns
1087.   On mutiny or hatching plot,
            And serves the new king England owns,

The red-head bully, blunderer, sot,
   Thick with curses, thick as his blood,   290
   Shot in the Forest, and well shot.
Shot ill or well, shot bad or good,
   That red king was his father's son,
   To keep in awe his robber brood;
Beauclerk. And so when he was dead and done   295
   Did Henry Beauclerk many a year,
   The shifty, patient, waiting one,
With little joy of his home gear
   But such content as may be told in
   The country's peace from year to year.   300
Now has good Hodge enlarged his holding
   To a quarter virgate in the strips ;
   Now a fair wife for arms' enfolding
Awaits his summons of the lips.
   Villein and neif they well may be,   305
   But that's your world which your mind grips :
There needs no other.   Wise is he
   Who works his patch and joys in it,
   With ankles hobbled, but mind free.
To better that may pass man's wit.   310

BOOK II

CURTMANTLE

BOOK II : CURTMANTLE

Anarchy.

LET mortal man make ready to weep
    At all times, ere good fortune flit !
No sooner was that king dug deep
  To lord his narrow earthen bed,
  Forthwith from donjon, tower and keep   5
Lift one by one a rascal head,
  And tongues were clackt, and whispers leapt
  Like spears of fire : " The kings are dead—
Up, chieftain, out ! "   Forth Sarum stept,
  Bishop and knight, and like a cock   10
  Clapt wings and crowed, as him which kept
Peter ashamed of gibe and mock
  For many a day ere he became
  His Master's gatekeeper and rock.
They rise, they flare with sword and flame   15
  Out and abroad the country over ;
  Nor, as when hawks fall foul, the game
And hedgerow finch may cower in cover,
  And very fieldmouse take to his hole,
  May Hodge get screen from his wind-hover. 20
Let lords of land take bloody toll,
  Let kings of it shed life like rain,

33   D

THE SONG OF THE PLOW

The land must have Hodge body and soul:
To it! To it! to work again!
    They skin the land, the castles rise,   25
    The castles fall; o'er Sarum plain
The quick fire runs, the quick hare flies,
    The Five Rivers flow red water;
    Brother bites brother traitorwise,
And Lust, which is War's eldest daughter,   30
    And Cruelty, which married Lust,
    Breed curious vice from furious slaughter.
Let Hodge encounter as he must
    To see his sons hung by the feet,
    To see their brains pockmark the dust,   35
To see their fair flesh made dogs' meat;
    And his raped daughter grinning grief,
    Naked and witless in the street,
Wreck of the lechery of a thief,
    Ransackt and shockt, deflowered and flung   40
    Out like a dirty handkerchief
To lie betrodden in the dung.
    Himseemed that Nature and the Air
    Had art and part these shames among;
The murrain festered, everywhere   45
    Was sheep-scab; this year was a drought,
    Next year the floods, all years despair.
And thus the reign of riot ran out
    With King and Empress up and down;
    A shout of triumph, then a rout: 50

34

CURTMANTLE

Then came King Death and took the crown,
　　To add it to his goodly batch
　　Of such memorials in Hell town.

A Man, Renew, man Hodge, with yelm your thatch,
1154.   Warm your chill bones, the hour is planned 55
　　When thieves of men shall meet their match:
There comes a man to hold this land—
　　A freckled man, blinking and squat,
　　A crook-kneed man of fidgety hand,
In an old cloak and a vile hat, 60
　　But Lord! a man! He had a prong
　　To rend the scum from the yeasty vat
Whose bubbles were men's breath, whose song
　　Was *Thine is mine!* and *I bleed! I bleed!*
　　Gasp of the poor or grunt of the strong. 65
Scutage. But of his ordering and good heed,
　　How he foiled his robber lords,
　　Buying shields as he had the need,
Taking their money to hire their swords:
　　Here is stuff for the Chroniclers, 70
　　Them that sweat deeds into words.
Little of such high policy stirs
　　Plowman Hodge in his green realm
　　Of grassy hills and junipers.
He spreads his straw, he pegs his yelm 75
　　To mend the thatch; he snuffs the breeze,
　　The wind comes warm; there's bud on the elm:

35

THE SONG OF THE PLOW

Out and about! Good sap to your knees,
　　Health to eye, to backbone marrow;
　　Rid your acres at your good ease,　　　　80
Drive your plow, weigh down your harrow
　　What time your head-bowed oxen trudge;
　　While cow's in calf or sow's in farrow
There's God in the sky to wink at Hodge,
　　And King Curtmantle his world to scan　　85
　　Here below; and he'll not budge
Tho' barons bicker and churchmen ban.

Clarendon.　Now to the beechwoods over the down,
　　Where deer are twice the worth of a man,
The King rideth to Clarendon;　　　　90
　　And Hodge may view him from the fields,
　　Him with his bad hat for a crown,
His tramping legions, horses and shields,
　　Mitred priests and their sacraments—
　　Such gapeseed the high world yields!　　95
Like toadstools dimpling in the bents
　　Rise in a night of miracles
　　Towns and villages of tents
(Hodge to Hob this wonder tells);
　　And of the prince of dark visage,　　100
　　Archpriest Thomas, riding the hills
Furtive before the King in his rage,
　　Who wrings his nails to see him there
　　And know his peer, with gage for his gage,

36

And craft for his craft. For he can stare   105
   With eyes unheeding, vacant, mild,
   As if he saw God in the air
Shap't like a man or naked child,
   What time his master fumes and mutters,
   Or pads the floor like wolf of the wild,   110
Mouthing impotence, froths and splutters,
   Thinks to cow him, cries to be rid
   Of the pest he is. But that cry he utters
Undoes full half of all he did.
   Desperate work there lies before ye,   115
   Strong Plantagenet, hoarded and hid ;
For that shaved poll a crown of glory,
   Martyr's light on his politics,
   Tapers and gold for his feretory ;
For you the smear of blood that sticks.   120
   Great doings at Clarendon !
   Nought to the man behind the quicks
Cutting his hunch, or out in the sun
   Slipping the plow-share thro' the flints.
   King or Bishop, it's all one   125
To goodman Hodge while the sun glints
   On jingling harness or crow's wing,
   And warms his back as he works his stints.

Ikenai.   Now let him learn the way of a king.
   It was by Clarendon, they say,   130
   This king out at his goshawking,

37

Riding in the cool of the day
  Up to the down, must fall love-bitten
  Before a maid called Ikenai,
A girl with a round face like a kitten,   135
  Gooseherding in the common pasture,
  With sky-blue eyes and hair sun-litten,
As slim as a boy in her smockt vesture—
  Young Ikenai, plain Hodge's daughter !
  But he must make himself her master ;   140
So men of his went out and bought her,
  Since he must have her by all means ;
  There was no way, her will was water :
The paramount must rule the mesnes.
  He did but as a king may do ;   145
  The child was cowed and made no scenes,
But took the use he put her to
  And bore the burden of womenkind ;
  Gave him a son, or maybe two—
But one was a man of his father's mind.   150
  And as for her, why, no one knows
  Ought about her, or ought can find,
Save she was Hodge's girl, a rose
  Flickt from the hedge for a man's breast,
  Fading the while his way he goes   155
And dropt mid-journey. Guess the rest :
  Here's enough of deeds in the shade.
  Better than many, tho' bad was best,
1189. This king was, and his end he made

CURTMANTLE

Even as his life had been.   He died   160
Old, ill, forsaken and betrayed
In his castle by Vienne's tide,
Warring upon his fine tall sons,
Beaten and beggared of all but pride :
That he had, to cover his bones.   165

Fool and Knave.

Now of his sons I have nought to say
(When fools are kings the wise pen runs) :
Richard the Minstrel, Yea-and-Nay,
A hawk the Archduke lured with his lime ;
Him that took life for a firework-day   170
And burnt himself out before his prime—
Nought of him, who lived and was dead
Ere Hodge knew him, for Hodge's rhyme.
And what of Lackland, slugabed,
That sold his kingdom to the Pope?   175
Little enough when all is said :
Trust him to hang, with enough rope.
Slugging he lost his Normandy
And penned his lords in narrower scope
Since they must choose where they would be 180
Masters, in England or in France.
There was his rope ; and the tall tree

1215.

Was Runnymede's where they made him dance
They called the tune, he needs must foot it ;
Well might Hodge take the play askance ! 185
For all the triumph that they bruit it
Brought little joy to him and his.

39

Charter of Liberties, they put it :
God knows it was not Liberty's.
   Liberty for a man to swing
   His villeins on his own park-trees !   190
Freedom to make freedom a thing
   Not to be hop't for !   If Hodge hears
   The pæan which the lawyers sing
'Twere well he'd wax to plug his ears.   195
   For this inspires their shrilling words,
   That lords have judgment of their peers,
And the terre-tenants—of their lords !
   Great hearing, Hodge, thy plow to speed
   The Barons' Carta Magna affords,   200
Wrung, with a rope, from Runnymede.

Hodge's
Affairs
   But Hodge, the Man upon the Hill,
   Hath other lack of instant deed,
Seeing in house a young child ill ;
   And he must after the reeve's wife   205
   To tell him why it lies so still,
And burns, and burns, and dare the knife
   To cut the blanket out of its throat
   And give it back the breath of life.
Or he must off to Halimote   210
   To hold, and be asham'd by no man,
   His right and title to hedgebote,
Or lay his lawful claim to common ;
   Or find John Stot a plain cuckold,

Or duck Madge Hern, the foul-mouthed
   woman,   215
Bleared, white and viperous, a scold—
   And what is Runnymede to him?
   And is King Richard dead and cold?
Or is King John King Satan's limb?
   Or the Pope innocent? Courage, verse,   220
   Here's an end. Make your tackle trim.
Times shall be better, ere they be worse.

BOOK III

BONACCORD

BOOK III : BONACCORD

The double Brand.

WHEN God first made this teeming earth
    He set a man and woman in it,
And bid them love and bring to birth
More of their kind to work and win it.
    To it they went. The sons they had   5
    Lived brotherly, but in a minute
They fell a-bickering—Cain went mad
And slew his brother, for that he
    Stood well with God. A logic bad
Taught him high hand a remedy   10
    For lack of grace ; and that is how
    Man covered pure Fraternity
In a bloody shirt. The weak must bow,
    And double-scored the brand of Cain,
    Burnt in the strong man's masterful brow   15
And where the little man's leg-chain
    Galls the thin flesh. A devil's dodge
    That was, by force of arms to gain
That which you have not earned and grudge
    Your neighbour, him that was your brother, 20

45

THE SONG OF THE PLOW

That earth-worm in his cast, poor Hodge.
Hodge and my Lord should love each other—
But how get at it ?   There's the twist.
The only man to solve that pother
Is your whole-hearted idealist   25
Who sees Truth naked.   We had one
And slew Him, God's son Jesu-Christ ;
And then twelve hundred years must run
Before another poet stood,
And saw the work in Eden begun,   30
As God had seen it, very good.

The gray   By mountain path and valley ford
Poet.   Came a gray poet in a hood,
With news for all from his sweet Lord ;
A barefoot poet in serge gown,   35
Our pleasant brother Bonaccord,
Sib thro' Assisi to the clown,
Upon the glebe, and as he saith
Sib to the wretch that wears the crown,
Since he loves all things, even Death,   40
And deems the man that gives his life
To serve his friends no waster of breath.
1221.   Now to this land where woe is rife
Amid the waving cornlands come
These sons of Francis and his Wife,   45
And see a shambles, and make a home,
And hush men's groaning till it cease,

And wake the blind and voice the dumb,
Crying abroad the Prince of Peace.
 Strange doctrine which a man may keep 50
 Beside him in his little ease !
How Brother Death and Sister Sleep
 Are out with him beside foul weather ;
 How Brother Ox and Brother Sheep
Share the same parentage together. 55
 He shall defend them under His wing,
 They shall be safe beneath His feather ;
Nor shall they fear ill fortune's sting
 Nor murrain's burn nor famine's bite,
 Nor greedy lord nor idle king, 60
Since all are blindworms in His sight
 Who made this world a garden-plot
 Where He might take His pure delight,
And weeps to see His aim made nought,
 By them he set upon the road 65
 And made so fortunate, they forgot
They must bear one another's load—
 But now the carrying falls to Hodge,
 While his high brother wields the goad.
A difference 'twixt *drudge* and *drodge* 70
 There is, as teaches a good scrip :
 The first's content his heart to lodge
In toil, and find strength in its grip,
 A slave to work ; t'other's a slave
 At work ; he slaves for fear of the whip. 75

'Twas Bonaccord came in and gave
  The heart again to English grist,
  And made a workman of a knave.
Now let the mill grind as it list ;
  The good grain grows as first it grew,   80
  Since Bonaccord makes Bonacquist.
Barefoot and laughing, two by two,
  Forth by the mountains and the sea,
  To sup on England's bitter brew,
Came those gray gowns from Italy.   85
  And this was all they had to teach :
  Thrice blessèd is Saint Poverty ;
As poor, yet making many rich,
  As having nought, possessing all.
  Stitchless, to folk without a stitch   90
They sang this life a madrigal ;
  And why our Lady chose an inn,
  And bare her Son in oxen-stall
(Because her kingdom was within
  As ours is too if we would choose it) ;   95
  And why Christ died—to drive this in,
Whoso would save his life must lose it.
  So to poor Hodge the broken serf,
  So to the outlaw, so to the stews, it
Flies fast and far, as o'er the turf   100
  Cloud-shadows and the sun hold chace.
  Even he who, gnawed by silver scurf,
Gropes for his way without a face,

The leper of the clacking boards
Warms to the gospel full of grace   105
That calls him brother of his lords
(Since God was made a poor girl's child).
Within his fretted flesh he hoards
The message from the Undefiled,
And bears his loathsome burden yet   110
A little longer, reconciled.
Broadcast is flung this holy net
That knits up all men in a band
Of common right and common debt
In what all men may understand.   115
They sing the gods denied to no man,
Whether he till or hold the land ;
Whether of Sarum use or Roman
The Church, these two her altar knows,
The One a child, the other Woman.   120

adonna. O You that cast like a shed rose
Your maiden grace and delicate pride !
Up to your Lord as incense goes
Your dawning womanhood undenied ;
And so He takes you for the spouse   125
Of Heaven ; and so you are His bride,
Mother of Men, your womb the house
Of this our Brother that was slain,
A King who for the love of us
Took up our nature and our pain !   130

Ah, Flower of Women, what woman born
  Grudges the heartache and the stain,
Knowing within your breast the thorn
  Of that your Son's torment and death,
  Or fronts the morrow's lowering morn   135
Uncomforted by your sweet breath ?
  Now thuswise Brother Bonaccord
  Or some gray visionary saith
From Dover Strait to Haverford,
  And thence across the midland shires,   140
  Until he strikes the cold sea-board
Where in the north men light the fires
  In belfries to warn off the Scots.
  Peace, not a sword, snug-wattled byres,
Not castles, builds from John o' Groats   145
  To the Land's End this Conqueror
  For his rope-cinctured hodden-coats.

The
Sowing.
    The grain was on the threshing floor
  When these newcomers toucht the land ;
  They purged the seed and added more,   150
And flung it broadcast, as the sand
  Is sown by carrying wind ; and some
  Fell among thieves, and some was banned
By them that sweep the table-crumb
  To dogs rather than Lazarus ;   155
  And some made stew and stye and slum
Fragrant with young-eyed hope. And thus

50

Their logic went : if God was flesh,
Then flesh was God, and God with us
Was fettered, and made sweet the mesh,   160
  With King and Hodge alike divine.
  Let Oxford now this new grain thresh
Until comes broadening like a line
  Of light far over a stormy sea
  The thought : " If this is brother of mine, 165
How comes it he is lord of the fee,
  With dogs to hound me to the field,
  While I, his villein, go unfree ?
What then ! I huddle in a bield
  On a dung floor among the rats,   170
  The mixen at the door my shield
Against the weather, and these slats
  Keep sun and rain from the straw bed
  Where I must pig it, man, wife, brats
All coucht like swine ! I'm suckt, I'm bled 175
  To work my brother's broad demesne :
  He fares abroad, and when I'm dead
My son, to herd where I have been,
  Must pay, my penury to get,
  Make my lord fat for leave to go lean ! " 180
Questions for Hodge ! Not yet, not yet ;
  Enwombed as yet, against the day
  When he and Redeless Richard met
Face to face—and the fool gave way.
Henry III. But now that lax-veined son of John 185

Lolled with his foreigners at play,
And built with what he had not won
   The great gray church embankt by Thames
   Wherein to store his carrion
When he had done with money and gems.   190
   And now the men who called him king
   Prove him and kingship empty names,
Fleecing the realm, to fiddle and sing,
   To strum the tunes of *Gai saber*.

Hubert de Burgh. One man stands up, and him they fling   195
Into the jail, to fester there.
   Hubert, too late Curtmantle's lore
   Upon his thieves you brought to bear ;
And all your doughty shoulders bore,
   Grosseteste, you greatest son of Hodge,   200
   Might never stem the tide of war.
Yet you were found an upright judge
   By Francis' sons and Dominick's,
   Seeking a shelter and a lodge
Out of the storm of politics,   205
   Which like a mighty waterflood
   Swept England bare, and left dry sticks
Behind its eddying smoke and blood.

Lewes, 1264. Of blood and smoke enough, good Muse !
   Of young corn trampled into mud,   210
Of Lewes Down above the Ouse
   Where Richard of Almain was pounded,
   And Henry learnt a foreign use

52

Sharper than any he had founded ;
  Of Simon Montfort's whip and sting,   215

esham,
65.
ward,
72–
07.
  Or Evesham where his life was rounded,
What came there out ?   A long-legged King,
  Who learnt of Simon, and had wit
  To know when sword had need to ding
And when to mount the mercy-seat,   220
  And his best work within his land
  To make himself no use in it.
He builded wiselier than he planned
  Who gave himself a Parliament,
  To find him money out of hand—   225
Which to his heirs, in the event,
  Became a tingling and an itch,
  Wringing their hearts to its intent,
Screwing them up to charter-pitch ;
  Which was for gentlemen a rock,   230
  Which was the staple of the rich,
And now is fallen a common mock
  When, hedging out its knaves and fools,
  It stays them not, but chockablock
With business, dies of its own rules,   235
  Bound hand and foot—while fool and knave
  Flap their wings, and the nation cools.
Hidden from thee, thou wise and brave
  Plantagenet, little loved in Wales,
  This crumbling of the architrave   240
Wherewith thou hopedst tie the pales

That fence about thy seigniory,
This holy island !   Nought avails
Her sacred girdle of the sea,
Nor welded chain nor smithied bolt   245
'Twixt thy degree and our degree,
If gangrene fester in the holt,
Or men long fretted by the gall
Learn the proud uses of revolt,
And old Saint Use no saint at all !   250
Work for thy Parliament hath Fate ;
And how it rose, and by whose fall
Stood face to face with thy estate,
And by long fanning of the wings
Of war stood sovereign, and of late   255
Hath taught the workers to be kings
And spurn it like a broken toy—
Hither I wend as the song sings.

Hodge.   Back now to Hodge and his new joy,
Profusely taught him, snugly treasured   260
As he goes trudging with his boy
The ruts their patient feet have measured
Since breeches covered innocence.
To serve his turn at work or leisure
He holds it fast, the dawning sense   265
That there's a God of simple folk,
A Woman for his reverence,
A Child she rears to bear a yoke.

54

In tilth, in mead, with sheep on hill,
Musing he stands, and sees the smoke   270
From village hearth rise up and fill
The blue air with a sharp wood-savour ;
And the dream comes and keeps him still,
That so may reek of him find favour
With that warm-bosomed Mother of God 275
Nursing her brave Son, herself braver,
Seeing she was woman as well as God,
And loved to give, and now must watch
The pains of manhood burn in God.
Hold fast thy gold beneath the thatch,   280
Thou son of man !   There's many a day,
And many a breathless plowing-match
On bitter acres ; long's the way,
And bloody are the milestones on it
Ere thou canst hear the Angel say,   285
" Take here thy throne as thou hast won it "—
And may be for thy gilded crest
And kingly sign, a cotton bonnet !

The Seed When two wan lovers breast to breast
f Hope.   Cling to each other beneath the moon,   290
Their wattled garret is a nest,
Their rags spell out the holy rune
Which makes them high priests of the night,
And drums their hearts to a rapturous tune,
The measure of their still delight.   295

55

THE SONG OF THE PLOW

Sheeted with gold their palliasse,
Since love has fired the straw with light ;
The hours like scented moments pass
  Wherein they love ; and when they sleep,
  Clinging together, each one has   300
The dream made fast and rooted deep,
  A budded roof-tree against dearth,
  A vine engraft, a fruiting slip
To make an orchard of the earth !
  So now hath Hodge in his poor hold   305
  A sapling stem of priceless worth,
Like to that rod wherewith of old
  Moses struck water from the stone ;
  A wand to turn his cap to gold
And draw thanksgiving from a groan.   310
  So stands he in this dawn of days
  As one who waits and is alone
In a forest, at four cross-ways,
  And hears the countless little noises,
  And hearkens what the woodland says,   315
Rustle of rabbit, clear bird-voices,
  Then out afar the cuckoo's call,
  Where on his ash-tree he rejoices
In sky, warm wind and sun for all.
  So heartens he, and looks beyond   320
  With ridded eyes, and sees how small
The shadowing wood, his fear how fond,
  The road how plain, how near the goal ;

BONACCORD

For that glad music seems a bond
'Twixt his soul and the over-soul.   325
    And so he takes his fardel up,
    And loves the world, and knows it whole !

Thus Francis mixt the stirrup-cup,
    And sped our Brother Bonaccord
    To proffer it for Hodge to sup.   330
And Hodge drank deep, and prais'd the Lord.

BOOK IV

THE BLACK PRINCE

BOOK IV : THE BLACK PRINCE

*Spring-time,
1327.*

WINTER is past, the birds a-wing
  Wheel in the plow's wake ; from the
   down
Throngs the innumerable carolling
Of lambs whose asking voices drown
 All clamour but the watery bleat   5
 That beckons each. The buds are brown
Upon the elm-tops. The glad heat
 Ripples along the hills' gray edges,
 And o'er the dewpond where the feet
Of wagtail print the little wedges   10
 Which mark his nodded harvestings
 For wife and children. In the sedges
By riverside the warbler swings ;
 And there midflood a rising trout
 Noses, then oars beneath his rings,   15
Then in a flurry swirls about.
 From the lord's woodland comes a cry
 Where swineherd watches snuffle and snout ;
Along the road you see go by,
 Pacing demurely on a mule,   20

THE SONG OF THE PLOW

The parson and his loteby—
His by snug practice, not church-rule.
　　All's well with Hodge these golden weeks,
　　After the folly of the fool
Was chokt in blood, and the fog-streaks　　25
　　That swathed the eyes of Berkeley's keep
　　Could not hide Edward's torture-shrieks.
He sowed and therefore had to reap ;
　　But goodman Hodge, by that red job,
　　Stood better, all his fellowship,　　30
When he, or Rob, or Hob, or Lob
　　Might freely hold his toft and garth,
　　Or get some schooling in his nob
If so he would, and see his hearth
　　Swept by free woman for free man ;　　35
　　For now the Lord of English earth
Must have what provender he can
　　To wage his wars and pay the knaves
　　Called out by ban and arrière-ban.
To enslave the French he freed his slaves　　40
　　In England, then their sons bespoke
　　For butcher's work across the waves.

Outlook.　Oh, busy highways full of folk,
　　Oh, pleasant days by countryside
　　Ere yet the dreadful pinion-stroke　　45
Brought the fell angel on our pride,
　　And made this land a charnel-house,

62

THE BLACK PRINCE

This land now laughing and young-eyed !
Hodge heeds the knights for whom he plows
    Ride forth to tourney in the lists ;   50
    The bannerols, the horns that rouse
The cattle in the river mists,
    The huntsmen and the dogs, the light
    Women with falcons on their wrists.
Darkling he sets, as well he might,   55
    My lord the Abbot at the chace,
    A pricker for his acolyte,
Antler and scut his meed of grace,
    Against yon pair of russet friars,
    That hedge-priest with his rapt pale face, 60
Who listens unseen heavenly choirs
    Sing the inheritance of the meek !
    Darkling he rakes the cowch and fires
The weedstack, and the trailing reek
    Smothers the glittering passing lords ;   65
    And where he heard the hunt-horn speak
He hears afar the clapper-boards,
    Stayed only while their master scratch
    Or falter wailing broken words
To passer-by for bite or snatch   70
    To help his travel—He and his sore,
    What are they but an awkward patch
Upon this world's wide pinafore,
    A makeshift, but the only wear,
    And good for Hodge's life or more   75

63

THE SONG OE THE PLOW

While fat year follows on fat year,
   And wages rise and corn is cheap,
   And a man owns his land and gear,
And with a wife and child to keep
   Hath wherewithal to front the day,   80
   Knowing his corn his own to reap !

Edward
III.
O young man mettlesome and gay,
   Who took our England in your trust,
   What is the price wherewith to pay
Your bellyful of sauce for lust,   85
   Your chivalry and magniloquence ?
   Ashes of ashes, dust of dust
On you who, swollen by your fed sense,
   Became the blind who led the blind,
   A bloated bladder of pretence.   90
Woe to you, wretch, that could not find
   In this good tilth your suffisance,
   But needs must grudge the golden rind
Of the sweet fruit that swells in France :
   There shall be bitter lines to score   95
   Ere England writes your chevisance !
For the third Edward was in store,
   This fate, to rob a lady's knee,
   To fall a-doting on a whore,
And see his fine sons' usury   100
   Cleave this good realm from end to end
   And drop it, for the husbandry

64

THE BLACK PRINCE

Of shrewder kings to patch and mend.
　Need for you, Canon of Chimay !
　Need for you, Chaucer, pleasant friend,　　105
To tell us good tales by the way,
　To make us merry while we bleed ;
　To sound the music of the fray,
Woo Amaryllis with a reed
　To venture from her leafy holt　　　　110
　Ere yet the spur shall gall the steed
Or the hired bowman notch the bolt !

valry
rance.　The hunt is up, the knights advance,
　And stallion King and princely colt
Fling heels up thro' the realm of France,　　115
　Pasturing their mettle.　They cut throats,
　They spit men's bodies on the lance,
They and the thieves they hire for groats ;
　They burn the green earth black as Hell,
　And Hob and Lob win more than botes　　120
When women's bodies are to sell,
　And dead men's purses come for the asking.
　Make what you can of it, Jehan le Bel !
Of brigandage as knighthood masking,
　Of young men taught the way of a beast,　　125
　Of Crécy and its evil tasking ;
Of Poitiers and the Prisoner's feast
　Where courtesy made more rude the chain :
　Make what you can of it, scribe and priest !

But look askance thro' Aquitaine   130
  And pass, or turn away and grieve
  Before Limoges and the red rain.

Black Black Prince, before you taught to reive
Prince.   There had been none of darker sword ;
         Immortal want made William thieve,   135
Craving of that which must be lord ;
  But you, my Prince, for wantonness
  Taught thieving to your conscript horde.
Homeward they come whom you did press,
  Soakt in the treasure earned with spears,   140
  French money and the French sickness ;
And home come you to untimely shears.
  But worse than any foreign scab,
  Poor Hob and Lob turned routiers,
To plunder kindred, ravish and stab,   145
  And spill broadcast their spawn obscene,
  Sowing in virgin the seed of drab,
That the unconceiv'd be born unclean.
  Prince, if indeed God gave you zest
  To spoil fat years, you earn'd the lean.   150

Black Lo, as you flung the topmost crest
Death.   Of all your glory, King, when you,
         Your sons and your light women, drest
For Garterdom in gold and blue,
  Held festival, was dug the grave   155
  Of Garterdom.   The next wave drew

66

And gathered mass, and o'er that wave
   The sky hung dusk and copper-red ;
   And there was a hush before it drave
Forth on its way of death and dread,   160
   To bring new heaven to new earth
   Over the charnels of the dead.
As in the East our light had birth,
   Thence came the darkness that must quench
   That light, and coming, lent wry mirth 165
To you, enharboured from the stench
   Of festering Florence, John Boccace !
   Wiling your ladies, lest they blench
To hear the groaning dead-cart pass,
   With long-drawn tales of love's sweet pain 170
   Under the olives on the grass.
And France, still smarting our domain,
   Must suffer now a blacker Prince,
   Who for one man by Edward slain
Slew a tenscore, and did not wince   175
   To cross the sea, but scarred this land
   With weals she has carried ever since.
Hither that angel with the brand,
   That flying lord men called Black Death,
   Courst with his bare blade in his hand, 180
And smote.   Such buffet stays men's breath.
   Men wait.   There is no prayer to say,
   Nor God to listen what prayer saith ;
For He has turned His face away,

To hide for a season, as He hid   185
When that absolving Flood had sway,
And all the filthiness men did
Under a vast unwrinkled sheet
Of waiting water was drown'd and rid.

Rain and At first it seemed He would repeat   190
Plague. That cleansing purge, when that He sent
  Unending rain, and whelm'd the wheat
In heavy ear. Saint John's tide spent,
  The rain began, and thence to Yule
  It hardly stopt, and thence to Lent   195
Continued ; but the Plague smote full
  Midway the floods, and set afloat
  The dead, and made a poison-pool
Of drownèd field and mergèd cote.
  There were no priests for houselling,   200
  Nor men to dig, so fiercely smote
The fever. Men stood whispering
  " Who next ? Is it I ? " And on the thought
  Came the dry ache and thickening
Like lead in the veins ; and sight was nought 205
  But a swim of dark. And men went mad
  And tore themselves, or ran and caught
Their wives, saying " Save me ! " or unclad
  Fled thro' the fields, or bit, as dogs
  Bite water ; or if wit they had,   210
Crept out of sight and lay like logs,

Covering their heads with sackcloth.   Still
The endless rain that steeps and sogs
The land, and swims the taint of ill
Broadcast ! To breathe it is to choke.   215
Men fly the valleys for the hill
And huddle, sodden by the soak,
Awaiting till the rising tide
Of water brim the carrion-smoke
Up to the crest.   John Stot's wife died   220
A Tuesday, when John Stot was gone
To work three hours.   The children cried
And pulled her gown.   The eldest one
Scolded and husht them.   " Look," said she,
" The pretty spot my finger's on.   225
'Tis like a gillyflower.   And see,
Here's another ! "   Then she stared
And stiffened, and lookt fixedly ;
And tho' they throng'd her knees she glared
Up at the rafters ; and the spot   230
Glow'd on another armpit bared.
Then all her troubles were forgot,
And there was left one out of five
To wait, but not to see, John Stot.
He was caught seeking priest to shrive   235
His soul, because he saw the mark ;
But there was no priest left alive.
The child sat there till it was dark
And all the pallid sleepers hidden ;

So still it was, the wild dog's bark,   240
Calling his mates to feast forbidden
  In the empty street, was sound of cheer,
  And his breath snuffling in the midden.
She slept, and when the gray did peer
  Between the slats, the glimmering bed,   245
  So still, so still, awoke wild fear
In her. She caught at the door and fled
  Into the street. A dog was there
  At his hot business with the dead,
And stay'd to watch her. The sick air   250
  Was fill'd with bellowing of the kine
  Unmilkt, and shrill and everywhere
The squealing of the unfed swine
  Made clamour. But the silent crew
  Behind their shutters made no sign.   255
A light rain fell, a chill wind blew
  Upon the one soul left astir
  In all the village. Pale sun threw
A watery radiance over her.
  She found her father in the lane   260
  Beside the church, where others were
As quiet as he—with his disdain.

  Hodge, not his master, took the shock
  Of this fierce ally of the rain,
Which smote the parson and his flock,   265
  Smote carter, shepherd, plowman, hind,
  Cut down the fogger at his stock,

And his good wife with wool to wind.
   It took the white monk in his cell,
   It took the black monk and his kind   270
Who labour in the garth and dwell
   Together in the cloister-bays ;
   Upon gray friar and pied it fell,
Taking them suddenly in the ways.
   It caught the outlaw on the heath,   275
   And chokt the minstrel with his lays.
It left the throne and mow'd beneath ;
   Its sword was pulpy in the shank
   With English blood ; the more its teeth
Bit, the more thirstily it drank.   280
   Men bore their own dead to the ditch
   And heapt them there. The whole land
      stank
Of death. Yet Hodge made out a hitch
   In justice, when this doom was done
   That smote the poor, and spared the rich. 285

After the Enough of havoc ! When the sun
Death.   Uprose and warmed this land again
   Full half the souls were dead and gone
Who had wrought there, and wrought in vain.
   Full half the souls were 'neath the sod,   290
   Dead of the ruin and the rain ;
And when priests cried him turn to God,
   Well might Hodge raise an impotent fist
   Against this despot with the rod

Who let the plague strike as it list.   295
  Well might he give his flouted soul
  To body's whim, live like a beast,
And lacking good cheer take to foul!
  And so he did, if we may trust
  His chroniclers, who see him roll   300
And wallow in the stye of lust,
  Sunk to the eyelids, a hog turned loose,
  Chousing the cider in the must,
Easing his hot flesh in the stews
  To lure his heart from fruitless sorrow.   305
  What boots it, he might say, to muse
To-day, if I must die to-morrow?
  Let me eat and drink, as bids Saint Paul,
  And leave the plow stuck in the furrow,
And let the ox starve in the stall,   310
  And let the land go by the board;
  The King has half, let him have all,
So that a wilderness call him Lord!
  They know not Hodge, nor yet his land
  In whose deep heart his own is stored;   315
They have not markt his careful hand
  Feel knee and fetlock, nor his eye
  Make loving cast o'er the thin sand
Or chalky slope where his goods lie.
  They know him not who know not this,   320
  His life is in his husbandry.
And where his life, there his God is.
  There were ten patient and resign'd

For one who howled his blasphemies ;
And for one swilling sot you'ld find   325
    A dozen serving of their saint,
    Walking his way, no look behind,
No fear to look before, nor faint
    At heart.   The land, said they, is sick,
    The beasts are starved.   A saw half quaint 330
Half desperate gives their grim ethick :
    " If *ifs* and *buts* were apples and nuts "—
    So runs it trippingly and quick—
" I'd sit at home and fill my guts."

Outcome.   And now a mercy forth from the evil   335
    Rayeth, to help him cleanse his ruts ;
And God hath served Him of the Devil,
    It seems ; for so the Plague works out,
    The lords of land grow sudden civil,
And Hodge hath no more need to lout   340
    And cadge for hire.   The land is sere
    For want of tillage.   Turn about !
Corn is dead cheap, and labour dear,
    Since few there be to labour or buy ;
    And vain for Bishop, King and Peer   345
With Commons men " Out, dogs ! " to cry.
    Statutes of Labourers break no bones,
    And breed no men the hoe to ply ;
Hodge is the master for the nones,
    The villein is become the free ;   350
    And now he hears the organ tones

Of greater music—minstrelsy
  By Bonaccord begun—which fills
  The waiting land from sea to sea.
Hear Langland from his Malvern Hills,   355
  Watching the Vale of Evesham brood,
  So fair, so rich in river and rills,
Dimpled with pasture, plow and wood,
  And lacking but the hearts of men!
  " Lord, who will show us any good ? "   360
Wyclif. Quoth he. One sounded even then
  A message for the stricken ears,
  Crying with voice and burning pen,
" Repent ye, for the Kingdom nears ! "
  And as to clear good ground of weed   365
  Men snatch the first fork that appears,
So this man wrought his work decreed,
  Serving himself of John of Ghent :
  Not the first Saint, nor last indeed,
To wield a dirty implement.   370
  Wyclif, you had your torch alight
  Wherewith to show our garment rent;
And some in its beam stood to fight
  Under your banner of Free Grace,
  And other some obtained a sight   375
Of God in Heaven, and saw His face
  Yprinted dark and stern of blee
  Within the Book's calf-covered case.
I know not how these things may be,

Nor to what men your gospel spoke,   380
  Save that Hodge was not of them. He,
Ere many a ring embarkt the oak,
  Cared nothing for the holy pages,
  Until the sun of Wesley awoke
And blazed on him the Rock of Ages.   385
  Rather he turned to Walsinghame
  Or Glaston his drab pilgrimages,
Adored the Winking Rood, or came
  Barefoot to saintly Thomas' shrine,
  Or where King Edmund's pious name   390
Proclaims his town with him divine.
  Yet this is true of you, brave priest,
  You shook the law of Mine-and-Thine,
Judging the greatest by the least.
  So to the headlands, in the lew   395
  Where Hodge sat at his noonday feast,
This message came, so old, so new,
  Sped by your preachers on the green :
  The land's for all men, not for a few,
And he the slave of slaves, I ween,   400
  Who makes himself his own villein,
  Self-maddened like the Gadarene.

As in the woodland after rain
  The birds pipe a more liquid note,
  So rising from his fever and pain   405
Tuneth good Hodge a mellower throat.

BOOK V

RAGGED STAVES

BOOK V : RAGGED STAVES

NOW, Crécy, is your fame forgotten,
    Your Black Prince smothered up in
      lead,
Your Edward gone, whose bones were rotten
Before his minion knew him dead,
    Or robbed his fingers of the rings :   5
    Now reigns King Richard in his stead,
To flare the ruinous wake of kings.
    Starry at first, on meteor path,
    He spurns the ground with his bright wings,
Earth for his washpot, air for his bath :   10
    Of Edward's harvest he must mow
    The whirlwind for his aftermath;
Since in this world 'tis ordered so
    That there is given to every wight
    An instant's choice of weal or woe,   15
To take or lose, to snatch or slight,
    And never another.   'Tis hit or miss,
    As lovers know, who kiss at sight,
Or doubting courage never kiss.
    You had your hour, Black Prince's son ;   20

Richard
II.

79

THE SONG OF THE PLOW

England rued with you your lachess ;
But what's for him by whom 'twas done,
(O Chaucer, hearken Langland's ruth !)
Who left you end what was begun
To ease a fed man's pricking tooth ?   25
Such heritage succession bruises—
And the heirs paid for it, in sooth !

*Unrest
afield.* Out in the lands the flying news is,
    " They bleed us, neighbour, look to it !
    The King's men squeeze the stones for juices, 30
Take from our very mouth the bit."
    Out in the lands among the sheep,
    Or where men stoop to hoe the wheat,
Moving in file ; who as they creep
    Pass on the word adown the line,   35
    " What saith the Miller ? Doth he sleep ?
What saith John Ball ? Gives he no sign ? "
    Be it cruddled frost or dripping thaw
    The spell, be weather foul or fine,
Be blackbird fluting in the shaw,   40
    Or wood pigeon with sudden clatter
    Breaking from boughs, or querulous daw
Assailing daw with empty chatter ;
    Not even when the North-West wind
    Shrills on the headland, and a smatter   45
Of snow skims on the iron rind
    Wherein he needs must delve and swink,

80

Hath Hodge a care ; nor doth he mind
The sullen gray of the snow-blink,
   With sickly yellow for its lights ;   50
   On darker matter must he think,
More cruel than any frost that bites.
   He hath a worm in his brain-pan
   That spawns by day and breeds o' nights,
The lurking brute in every man   55
   Which feeds on lust, and wakes to feed
   When that the heart is stirred to fan
The blood to passion, rage or greed.
   He had a flinty road to plod
   Who let that beast wake up to its need.   60
ote. Warm a man's heart, you move the God
   To sing your pleasure as you mete it ;
   Break a man's heart, and there's a clod
Shap't to your bidding as you beat it :
   Wound a man's heart, you loose the brute   65
   To tear your own heart out and eat it.
Hot blood surged upwards from the root
   Of evil in him, a light scar
   Turned to red rage from head to foot
Hodge, who is not a man of war,   70
   And fights not, save with his own beast—
   (An Ephesus is never far
From any son of woman, least
   From one so vulnerably plann'd).
   Hodge raises neither bill nor fist   75

On him who'd oust him from the land—
　Nay, rather sets his teeth and thins
　His lips, and spits upon his hand,
And works the glebe ; and sometimes wins
　His way by his dumb patiënce,　　　　　　80
　Incredible to weaker chins,
Or hotter heads, or quicker sense.
　So they who grudge his land make Law
　Their friend, on whose august pretence
They hold him, such his simple awe　　　　85
　Of custom and the Historic Present !
　He fits his judgment to a saw :
Possession's nine points.　Such is the peasant
　Who had land once, and now has none—
　Not even the waste where crows the pheasant,
Nor the bare road where motors run.　　　91

*Villein
and Free
Labourer.* Now, in the day we are coming at,
　With war's ill ending bad begun,
Hodge, it is said, was waxen fat,
　His wages rising and corn falling ;　　　95
　Yet there were men to make of that
More use than he, with no chain galling,
　To tie them to a lord's pinfold—
　Unlanded men at no lord's calling,
Who shifted, and their labour sold　　　100
　Where money was best and work went faster;—
　But waxing fat, like him of old,

He flung, they say, and kickt his master.
   I know not, I, how fat he waxt,
   Where learnt to kick and court disaster :   105
He saw his neighbour's bonds relaxt,
   His neighbour free to work or play,
   Himself still bound to his vill and taxt
Because he held on his old way—
   While Hob, become Free Labourer,   110
   Took his good four penny a day.
He loathed his bond, but could not stir
   While bondage was the parchment scrip ;
   Yet he snufft freedom in the air,
And felt great words light on the lip—   115
   Blown to a flame by thee, John Ball,
   Prentice of Francis' fellowship—
Which cried the land the fee of all,
   Master and man, and cat and mouse,
   With God for squire and Heaven for hall, 120
And Hodge within his wattled house
   (Since Adam delved and Eva span)
   Lord of his mess of beans and souse
As of his haunch my gentleman.
   For why ! The good Lord gave the earth 125
   Profit to be of him who can
Best husbandry ; of such broad girth
   No man need shun the swing of Fate :
   Let a man work, then face with mirth
His present enemy in the gate.   130

THE SONG OF THE PLOW

Out on the air like fumes of wine
Which fill the nose and fire the brain
Floated the sense of love divine
    Which had made man in his own shape,
    And set no bounds of Mine and Thine   135
Whereby the wastrel might escape
    The burden of his goliardise,
    Or where God lookt for man plant ape.
Tongues. This land set in her cloudy seas
    Consider now as full of tongues   140
    Whose words are carried on the breeze
Afield and shape themselves in songs
    Throbbing responsive to the plow,
    Or scattering fireflakes as the prongs
Toss reeking dung ; " Come, tell me now,   145
    When Adam delved and Eva span,
    Who was lord and who was theow,
And where was then the gentleman ?
    And who's my lord drives me afield ?
    And where am I left in his plan ?   150
He takes the chrism.   Unannealed
    Go I, with scrapings of the pot,
    Dishwater, parings of the peeled
Fruit, by my pains and ordering got ! "
    The song soared high, fierce ran the speech 155
    From green to green, from knot to knot
Of gaunt-eyed men.   Let bishops preach
    Peace upon earth !   Plain men will wink.

It skills not temperance to teach
To him still drunk with last night's drink.   160
   Now gathered men in ragged bands
   And raised a chant to make them think
Who had drained the green sap from the lands.
   " With whom d'ye hold ? " it ran. " Grind
      small !
   Trust ye John Schep, with us he'll stand. 165
Our day is coming, quoth John Ball."
   " Let Jack now turn his miln aright,"
   It said, " the Lord shall pay for all.
Let skill serve will and right win might ;
   But if right lose, God greet you well,   170
   Then is our miln all misadight.
Yet wit you, John hath rung the bell :
   Take you the tidings ; fly, lad, fly ! "
   Far and wide, o'er field and fell,
As leaves are caught it whirled on high ; 175
   In every market-chafferer
   A hot thought lit from eye to eye.
They held their courts of Piepowder,
   But little guessed what dusty feet
   Ere long would tramp by London tower 180
And drag out Canterbury to meet
   The woe he had dealt, not meaning ill,
   Being a fool and not a cheat.
Over the fleeces at Weyhill,
   At Oxford for Saint Frideswide, 185

THE SONG OF THE PLOW

Across the Fens wherefrom men fill
Saint Giles's fair at Lammastide,
    The flying word streamed like a star
    That breaks from Heaven, and fiery-eyed
Holds the earth breathless. Wide and far   190
    It flew afield, and tinged the mind
    With the red nutriment of war.
It dried the soul, as a hot wind
    Withers a heath to kindling-wood,
    And soon that panting land and blind   195
Is sheeted in a roaring flood
    Of flame which flies a ragged mane,
    And races, ravening for food,
Leaving behind it a black plain.

Poll Tax,   This was the stroke that fired the stacks   200
1378.   Of kindling stored in Hodge's brain :
To pay their war they set a tax
    On every head the country through,
    On lesser as on broader backs ;
And finding little gain, anew   205
    They plied the assise with sharper zest
    For girl unreckoned, old wife too,
Or baby nozzling for the breast ;
    And found their foreign war apaid
    In opening up a hornet's nest.   210
For as one suddenly dismayed
    Looks at his own familiar place

86

Aghast, and cries, " I am betrayed ! "
To ease, if not his heart, his face—
   From Hob to Lob the message flies   215
   Of injury in a common case.
A flare of red across the eyes,
   A swelling neck, or back a-bristle,
   And kings are wary if they are wise,
And send a smooth priest with an epistle   220
   To promise remedy for wrongs.
   But Redeless Richard whet his whistle
For braver notes than John Ball's songs,
   And sent a Justice down to Fobbing,
   To whom Hodge spake—but not with
      tongues.   225
Bampton, Commissioner, came tax-jobbing,
   And Essex met him, armed with bills.
   Bampton must needs give over his robbing,
And take, first fright, and then to his heels.
   Down came Trailbaston and my Lord   230
   To learn what like a drubbing feels ;
And Hodge drew blood, with scythe for sword,
   And raised a pale head on a pike,
   First standard for his ragged horde
Whereof this land knew not the like   235
   Until that day.   And now afield,
   Essex across the river-dyke
Calls Kent to arms.   Out in the Weald
   They cut the hay ; but now the scythe

bbing in
ssex,
81.

Has redder work.   The tocsin pealed 240
Over the water to Greenhithe
    Runs faster than king's messenger.
    It rings an end to teind and tithe
And rocks the keep of Rochester.
    Crawling they mass, and like a tide 245
    Float over land the scum and scour,
The offal of the magnified,
    Waste of their waste, and excrement
    Of their consumèd place and pride.
After the Castle the Church went, 250
    And after Church went monastery ;
    And Hodge in Surrey as in Kent
Learnt one good use of seigniory,
    Which cools the blood by blood-shedding.
    They braved the Mass at Canterbury ; 255
And now the Wearer of the Ring
    Hears himself called for by harsh throats—
    " Give us out Judas, the foul thing
That sold his Lord for a handful of groats ! "
    Out of the West and out of the Fast 260
    The tide of rage rises, and floats
A sea of drab as thick as mist,
    With here and there an angry head
    Uptost, and here and there a fist ;
And like a drowning withy-bed 265
    The pikes dip as the sea of blood
    Surges and creams—and drab is red.

The Prior of Bury took to the wood,
   And Candish, Lord Chief Justice, ran :
   There swayed a boat upon the flood,   270
A woman held it, stern and wan.
   She pusht it out, with " Swim, dog, swim ! "
   And so they got him, a writhen man
Biting his nails.   The end was grim
   When the Prior was caught in his own clips.
   Laid for poachers, they took *him;*   276
And Land and Church seal fellowships
   When Prior and Justice hob and nob
   Pike high, and dead lips kiss dead lips
And make mad mirth for a louting mob,   280
   The which, if spilt blood taught it revel,
   From higher heads had learnt its job,
And a man's kinship with the devil.
   And so in Bury's market place
   Found Bury's reverend lord his level.   285
Yet marvel is his foes found space
   To remedy the ills that turned them
   From serfs to beasts.   To mend their case
They dragged the charters out and burned them
   Which made them so ; and whom they slew 290
   Were they who first enslaved, then spurned
      them—
The lawyers that the charters drew,
   The jurors of the cruel assise,
   And all his friends who backt that crew,

THE SONG OF THE PLOW

John of Gaunt's of the dead-fish eyes. 295
  And this red work done, and this ridding,
  Hodge, England over, "London!" cries.
London. With one consent, on no man's bidding,
  Like a tide gathering weed and scum,
  From tithing, hamlet and lone steading 300
The ragged legions surge and hum :
  Full half of England on the road
  To tell the King occasion's come.

"John the Miller hath yground small,
  The King's Son of Heaven shall pay for all. 305
  Beware or ye be wo,
  Know your friend from your foe :
  Have enough and say Ho !
  And so we bid you call."

King
Richard. O child of ruth, now like a God, 310
  And now a shell for fiends to inhabit !
  Who bring to the stress a broken rod,
You had your hour but would not grab it.
  Nay, you were pledged. Your faith you
    broke.
  Hodge opens you his heart. You stab it. 315
For in these days of blood and smoke,
  Of fire and shout, of singing bands,
  When London streets are chockablock
With gaunt fierce faces and toss'd hands,

And royal Savoy falls to dust   320
Before the flame, and nothing stands
Wherein you have been taught to trust—
What do you make of your kingship,
O child of ruth, but what you must?
A moment's glory of the lip,   325
A moment's vision—then both pass,
And you have let occasion slip,
And misery is as misery was!

1381.   Yet paid his poll-tax with his poll
Legge the arch-thief; now at his Mass   330
Fell Canterbury, condemned to toll
With his heart's blood and strung entrails
The passage of his craven soul;
Now last the moneyer, Robber Hales,
Fell battered by the Ragged Staves;   335
And three gray heads on three wet pales
Stared at the fires thro' glazed eye-caves,
Ere you, King Richard, kist the shrine
And went to meet your rebel slaves.
Lo, dusty air in summer shine!   340
Banners in Smithfield's grassy space,
The hordes in drab, the white Ensign
When Hodge and King are face to face.
And then the sudden flash you had
Which was your instant's hint of grace!   345
If you seemed spirit more than lad,

A spirit of fire, a son of light,
Thro' whose clear skin the blood throbb'd glad,
Blame not your dupes who heard your bright
Clarion, "With whom d'ye serve ? *Par Dieu*,
I am your leader ! " Fool, what spite   351
Made you a liar ? Had you been true
And they free as you promised, say,
Had England not been glad of you ?

1399.   God knows you paid ! And so did they   355
Who took your word, and on your bail
Gave over victory on the day
When it was theirs, that they might hail
A King of the English—for an hour !—
Who had Occasion by the tail   360
And loosen'd hold in midmost stour
To lord it King of England still,
Until a starker wrest the power
And drain your blood to drive his mill.
And as for Hodge, betray'd, befool'd,   365
Let him get back to field and vill,
Adone with warring, his blood cool'd,
His swords turned sickles, and his clubs
Flails, while the wheels he over-rul'd
Grind him again, and sluice their hubs   37c
And slake their heat in blood of men.
He earns a drubbing who half drubs.

BOOK VI

DRENCHED ROSES

BOOK VI : DRENCHED ROSES

L ORD, what is man that for one's sake
  Ten thousand more should stab and
   bleed,
 And twice ten thousand hearts go ache
Ere he can slack his lickerous need
 Of sceptre, crown and ermine cope   5
 For garnish of him ? What indeed
Pretender, King, Pope, Antipope
 To us, each girt by his own cage,
 Despot in his own cinctured scope,
Each with his private wars to wage ?   10
 Must he that hath the call of love
 Upon him, or a holy rage
The stubborn creaking plow to shove
 Thro' stony acres, bread to win,
 Let it all go, made nothing of,   15
While Edward of March be out or in,
 Or Henry doubtful on his perch,
 Or Charles a Saint or Man of Sin ?
O God of Nature-out-of-church,
 How long wilt Thou let three or four 20
 In Thy Name leave the rest alurch ?

95

THE SONG OF THE PLOW

1399–
1461.

When Richard's crown King Henry wore
   Fared England better ?   Or when he
   Gave up the realm he had bargained for
And a fifth Henry took the fee,   25
   How stood she then, a dicer's throw
   For ruffling gamesters oversea ?
Young men were taken from the plow
   And taught to play their wild-cat tricks,
   To seam with hate an open brow,   30
And serve the end of politics,
   Which is to line your nest rookwise
   By filching of another's sticks !
The joy of the knees, the pride of the eyes,
   The call of the reins which lures us on   35
   To find an earthly paradise
Where man and maid are knit in one—
   Whose is this life that we must throw it
   Mere tribute to some mother's son ?
Teach us man's worth, that we may know it, 40
   Who, being alone in power to lift
   Above his nature, sinks below it !
If kings are nought, men have no shift
   To know them so, who have no voice
   In making kings, themselves adrift,   45
Marshall'd and handled like the toys
   Of chess-players.   On kings' demands
   They make of shame a witless choice,
Dipping in shame their hireling hands,

Crying out shame with bidden breath. 50
I. Lo, in their fire the Maiden stands !
And lo ! they hound her to her death,
  And end a century's brigandage,
  Themselves a prey to the brigands' teeth.
'Twixt Holland's greed and Warwick's rage, 55
  'Twixt Tiptoft's craft and Suffolk's guile
  Slipt in the Merchant of his age,
ward The King with budded lips asmile
  And eyes aglitter for his meat,
  Who egg'd the vile to bite the vile, 60
And watcht them grapple from his seat
  On high, and leisurely, with his hook,
  Fisht in their lordships, and made feat
His bed with stolen wool ; and took
  Shore's wife, the fat and smooth and white, 65
  To be his joy.—While England shook
Yet from the brunt of men in fight,
  And Henry died alone and mad,
  In larded women his delight
This sleek and prosperous tradesman had. 70
  How shall I sing that strife of thieves ?
  When thieves fall out wise men are glad,
And set to making up their sheaves.
  Upon the ruins of his house
  Sits Edward, and the County Reeves 75
Find not their office onerous ;
  For never a Parliament has he

97   H

Since county lords played cat and mouse ;
But rules as snug as fish in the sea,
   Despot and heedless, without peers,   80
   With crookèd Richard presently
To watch the chicks his pale wife rears
   To carry on his name and line.
   What shall they carry on but tears ?
1450.   Poor Jack Mend-all, it was not thine,   85
   With Men of Kent to nerve thy knees,
   To disengage the tortured twine
Of England's heart-strings, tho' thy pleas
   Brought battle over London Bridge
   And hanged Lord Say ! This land's disease 90
Call'd for a knife, and not a midge,
   To let bad blood, not to inflame
   The sick tissues of Privilege ;
And ere thy day of reckoning came,
   Poor Jack, with twist not to be mended,   95
   The Lords were at each other's wame.
And so the Norman's line is ended,
   And Magna Carta swampt in gall,
   And the long-legg'd King's wit expended
In vain, who hoped to build a wall   100
   'Twixt greedy vassals and their prey !
   For now's no Parliament at all ;
And all are gone the burning way
   Of hate and grudge ; and once again
   The King is up in lonely sway,   105

DRENCHED ROSES

And a new Conqueror's come to reign
  By little but a sword's pretence,
  Crown'd in the field, with Crouchback slain.

e and
oses. Good Hodge, who work, not stab, for pence,
  And munch your bacon on the down,   110
  Your masters cry your common sense
And own you honest, tho' a clown.
  Say they, He's temperate, he's chaste,
  He loves a wife, tho' she's his own ;
He works the day through which we waste,   115
  Splaying abroad like gadding bramble :
  What more would he have, with virtues braced
'Gainst lack of substance, sans preamble
  Of privilege his ills to cure ?
  True 'tis you hire no man to gamble,   120
Prove your black white or bastard pure ;
  Nor if you tempt the Deadly Seven
  Have you the wherewithal to insure
That what you do shall not be given
  Against you in a latter bill   125
  When they cast up accounts in Heaven.
To you, then, England's England still
  Tho' trampling knights break down your closes.
  The sun comes up behind the hill
While Warwick crowns one or deposes   130
  As battle swings.   With earth to fight,
  You had no lot with the drencht Roses.

THE SONG OF THE PLOW

1455,
May 22. When in Saint Albans Henry pight
His banner, and the gutters drank,
Full May was in, all flower-bedight,   135
And Hodge a-sowing of the brank
Out in the strips of champion-ground,
Or waist-deep in the marshes rank,
Ridded the gutters.   Anon came round
His friendly foe, grown masterful,   140
Burnt him his wheat, and harvest crown'd
1460,
July 10. *His* fighting year—while Nene ran full,
And that was done in half an hour
Which twice ten years could not annul.
Dec. 30. In the dark day by Wakefield tower   145
When York, ta'en like a fish in a net,
Lost his fond head, and had his power
Mockt in a paper coronet,
Below his pallid blood-stuck brow
Grinning in death the teams were set   150
Beyond the walls—that Hodge might plow.
March
29. Or Towton Field by Ferrybridge,
That Feast of Palms 'mid whirling snow—
How stood the township on the ridge ?
Serv'd they the Mass in Saxton ?   Nay,   155
They heard the din with scarce a fidge
Of shoulder, or a wink that way !
No man of Hodge's kin sped shaft
Or pusht a pike in that affray.
1464,
May 15. And when in Heaven the glad sun laught   160

100

And glitter'd in the Devil's Water,
Where many a lord drank his death-draught,
And drain'd was René's haggard daughter,
    The hills about were white with sheep,
    And the larks thrill'd above the slaughter. 165
Across the land the slow days creep ;
14.   Another spring is in ; the mist
    Smothers the pastures where must keep
Warwick, Kingmaker, his last tryst.
    Him he put up, and now would down, 170
    Proves himself stauncher agonist,
14. And strikes a blow by Tewkesbury town
    Which ends the Roses' biting match,
    And leaves him lonely in his crown.
Enough ! The evil viper-hatch 175
    Spawn'd by the Black Snake of Anjou
    Is well-nigh spent. Upon the latch
Time sets his hand, to flood with new
    Large air the stiving cloister-garth
    Wherein, friend Hodge, they hobbled you. 180
You stand up free upon your hearth,
    Adone with boones and such old gear ;
    You shelter in your own poor barth,
You work your way from year to year ;
    And work is plenty, well apaid, 185
    The seasons generous, corn not dear.
Well may you court your blue-ey'd maid
    And teach her how to make a man ;

The God of Nature finds that trade
Better than butchery for His plan.   190
　　Yet there are signs to give you pause
　　If you have wherewithal to scan
Cause in effect, effect in cause.

Signs.　　What think you of this crawling sea
　　Of grass that yearly narrower draws   195
The cantle left to husbandry ;
　　And as the sheepwalks come to grips
　　With tilth, wherein your labour's fee,
How shall you guard your acre-strips
　　While the flock masters wax apace ?   200
　　And what within you's in eclipse,
And where is now the morning grace
　　You felt of old when Bonaccord
　　Came with the glory on his face,
The light of Mary and her Lord ?   205
　　Where is the truth which Langland cried,
　　That Doing will save and not the Word ?
Once you had that, and more beside,
　　And hoarded it like secret pelf,
　　The which a man, if ill betide,   210
Might slip within the mantel-shelf,
　　A little store of ultimate gold
　　Wherewith to feed and warm himself.
And now the thing is stale and old ;
　　Your rickety gods creak in the cranks   215

Which set them wink ; your shrines are cold,
Your angels in their painted ranks
  Are flaking ; mildew and the worm
  Are busy with their spindle-shanks :
So all such gear must find its term !   220
  See your gross monks behind their walls,
  Fed neighing horses, high with sperm,
Kissing kept wantons in their stalls,
  With all their lands let out to hire,
  And all their parchments black with galls. 225
O barren land, once hearts' desire,
  Dead Gods and dead religionists !
  Where is a man to bring new fire
And burn these muck-heaps, rend these mists ?
  He is at hand ; but you, my Hodge,   230
  Were never much for monks and priests.
They come and go, but you don't budge ;
  Lip-service to the altar-flame
  And censer-smoke you give, but judge
The chief of Saints is him you name   235
  Old Use-and-Wont, which was and is,
  And is to come, always the same.
And find you Caxton's trade amiss
  In Westminster, where with his types
  He'll reel you books out of a press   240
As fast as you can warm your tripes
  With nappy ale ?   Consider well
  Of his invention over your swipes,

103

If it will stop at books to sell,
    Or news to sell—or trade in lies,   245
    Having found out a fœcal smell
May be the best of merchandise ?
    Foresee the Masters of the Bray,
    Merchants of clamour and greedy eyes,
And the young men who take their pay   250
    And buzz and trumpet carrion,
    Dungflies at a ha'p'ny a day,
Before you'd seal what Caxton's done.
    I think had he the gift to see
    His labour's end, he had tied a stone   255
About his neck and sought the sea,
    He and his press, and so deserv'd
    Better of men, it well may be.

Half Way, 1485. Four hundred years since Harold swerved
    At Senlac !   A new conqueror   260
    Stands where the Norman's bow uncurved,
Adone with thieving maskt as war.
    Four hundred years are yet to fill
    Ere Hodge stand at the open door
1884. Of Parliament, and foot the sill   265
    Past which the limits of his hold
    May be enlarg'd to what he will.
Not towers nor circlets of bought gold
    Hath he in need, nor shall he find ;
    But portion in the weald and wold   270

Where he hath wrought time out of mind.
  His gaunt hillside, his stony fields,
  His trees distorted by the wind,
The swept white grasses, the rough bields
  Of rock which stand for bower and byre,   275
  His endlong toil and his thin yields—
These are the bourn of his desire,
  Bought by a toll of sweat and tears,
  Bought by his wrong and shameful hire
Through twice four hundred stricken years.   280
  I look and see the end of it,
  How fair the well-lov'd land appears;
I see September's misty heat
  Laid like a swooning on the corn,
  I see the reaping of the wheat,   285
I hear afar the hunter's horn;
  I see the cattle in the ford,
  The panting sheep beneath the thorn!
The burden of the years is scor'd,
  The reckoning made, Hodge walks alone,   290
  Content, contenting, his own lord,
Master of what his pain has won.
  Grant me to reckon and rejoice,
  And be thou there to say, Well done,
O wellspring of my singing voice!   295

BOOK VII

THE DESPOTS

BOOK VII : THE DESPOTS

Bring rue and hyssop to asperge
The chantry-tomb of bygone years !
Unto my song, become a dirge,
O Fount of Pity, lend thy tears :
King Richard's fall at Bosworth rang
A people's death, to wakeful ears.

1485,
August.

NOW Sirius has bared his fang
    Over the earth, and on the rim
    Of the burnt acres ominous hang
The flickering air-waves ; sight is dim
    And breath a labouring while Hodge reaps   5
    The wheat, and his girl after him
Bends to the flatten'd swathes and heaps
    The golden armfuls into stooks.
    The work goes on while the sun creeps
Atop the hill of noon ; then hooks   10
    And sickles lie beside the sheaf,
    And men turn to the water-brooks.
O silent days of winking leaf
    And swooning hillside, when the birds
    Are dumb, and Reynard the arch-thief   15
Lies grinning at the huddled herds !

THE SONG OF THE PLOW

Rest in the thicket, man and wife,
  Drink deep your mess of whey and curds,
And watch askance the tide of life
  Brim to the flood.   There, in the shade,   20
  Your lad and lass with hot thought rife !
Her smock reveals her budded maid
  And draws his manhood to her bosom :
  Now let him woo, nor be afraid
To judge himself the microcosm ;   25
  For all the kingdoms of this earth
  Shall not afford him fairer blossom
Than maidenhead for manhood's worth.
  And now's his time, ere kings put in
  Rude commentary on rustic mirth !   30

Another harvest is to win ;
  And northerly, across the shires,
  On Radmore Plain the battle din
Drives Richard after his dead sires,
Henry   And makes your master one who knew   35
VII.   To wait upon his own desires,
And treat no man as false or true,
  But so much handsel for his grist,
  Held (as a Christian by a Jew)
Blasphemer or co-religionist   40
  According as conditions fare.
  Here thrones the Tudor as he list,
With his poucht eyes and wisps of hair,

110

Over the ruins of dead things,
And raking for his profit there   45
To found a despot line of kings ;
With little of Gaunt except his guile,
But wit enough to take the swings
Of Fortune without surge of bile—
He saved that for his son to spend   50
Along with his heapt money-pile.
This was a man without a friend,
A ruthless man, and yet a just,
Who had a broken realm to mend
And gave it peace, and won its trust   55
Because he serv'd it with his brains,
And eas'd his own thro' others' lust.
But as a land sick with long rains
Teems in the embraces of the sun,
And feels his jet in all her veins   60
Like fire and wine a glad course run,
So that the soakt and staring sod
Glows to a resurrection,
And every tree of flowering rod
At every joint puts out a knop   65
Until in living green the wood
Is garmented from stem to top—

The New Way. Now burgeon'd out this island realm
In factory and school and shop.
Great ships deck-loaded to the helm   70
Brought in Venetian spicery,

And took back wool enough to whelm
The world in fleeces oversea ;
   But other kinds of ware than these
   Men cheapen'd from Low Germany :   75
Erasmus with his quiddities
   Of God and Fate and man's Free Will,
   What time he tastes the world as 'tis
At high tables, and finds it still
   Most tolerable, for the tolerant.   80
   Now Greek comes in for who has skill,
And readings in the Testament,
   Of whether Faith will save, or Works !
   The Orient floods the Occident,
With Byzaunce fallen to the Turks ;   85
   Luther unlimbers tongue and pen
   To sear what evil remnant lurks
Of the fond dreams of ancient men—
   But little enough have such to say
   To Hodge seed-sowing in his fen.   90

The Old Way. Hodge labours on his antick way,
   Working his strips of champion land :
   He plows, he sows, he teds his hay,
He swims his mead with river-sand ;
   He pastures on the common grass   95
   Week in and out ; he cannot stand
To see the questing carvels pass
   Before the wind, a glory of white

THE DESPOTS

Upon the gray sea's emptiness ;
Or watch them top the edge of light   100
    And be no more than a wandering name
    Heard in the day and lost at night.
To him the West wind brought no fame
    Of Greenland or still Labrador,
    When Cabot home to Bristol came   105
And the old world knew one world more ;
    His heart beat not to hear the horn
    Shrill from the East the open door.
Clouted and patcht, a shred forlorn
    Pickt from the earth, as from the rib   110
    Of the first man was woman born,
There stand you, fibre of the glebe,
    The very hue and savour of it,
    With beast and bird and flower sib !
The lords of the world will make their profit 115
    Of you and yours ; but like a gland
    You hold a juice, and cannot doff it,
The sweet secretion of the land.
    New men rise up, the fortune-makers,
    And buy your heavy foot and hand ;   120
You are computed with the acres,
    But you abide, and they must go,
    The hatchment of the undertakers
The only title they can show
    That once they lorded it as stout   125
    As any sinner here below.

THE SONG OF THE PLOW

So you withstood the flurry and rout
    Of shifting lordships and new squires,
    Prepar'd to pull the lock devout
To whom obeisance requires :   130
    Yet these new men might well awaken
    Old Use-and-Wont to new desires !

New Men. Gresham and Paget, Russell, Bacon
    Take place of Scales and Tibetot ;
    Cavendish wins of Ros forsaken,   135
And Cecil adds to what he had got ;
    Boleyn is rising to be a lord ;
    Grosvenor is rich and Scrope is not.
Riches need funding ; soon the hoard
    Is buried in your English soil :   140
    Your new squire, Hodge, seeks new reward,
A quicker answer than your toil.
    " Leave plowing to the faint-wit school,
    Adone with tenants and turmoil
Who cheat their lord and call him fool   145
    For being easy !   I'm for sheep,
    Turn all to grass and breed me wool."

Enclo-sures. Before you know it grass-lands creep
    About you, and the hedgerows lean
    To fence you in : then, " What's to reap ? 150
And what do these on my demesne ?
    Who is this empty-handed shirker ?
    And whose this hovel on my green ? "
So here is Hob, who was a worker,

Thrown out to skulk along the ditch,   155
  A broken man, a hedgerow lurker,
His children thieves, his wife a bitch ;
  A scab upon the Commonwealth,
  Prick of an everlasting itch
Which neither Boards of Public Health,   160
  Nor Trade, nor Local Government,
  Nor soft hearts doing good by stealth,
Nor pulpit summons to repent,
  Nor docketings of chronic cases
  Can stay from miserable vent.   165
Open your hearts, not save your faces,
  Or there'll be brisker work to-morrow,
  Snug gentlemen with country places !

Henry
VIII. Old Henry goes, to no man's sorrow,
  Young Henry comes with high fanfare,   170
  And like a fed horse spurns the furrow ;
He must be serv'd with love or war.
  He takes his fill of knightly frays,
  Prancings in Flanders or Navarre ;
And as for women, Rumour says   175
  He never had one to his mind
  Though he had twice-three wedding-days.
Here was a prince of Nero's kind
  Who loved his lust, yet must be sure
  He had the waiting world behind   180
To cry him up its cynosure.

Slave of his own abounding zest,
He hunted every lickerous lure,
Hailing the latest for the best,
   And knotting as he went the strands   185
   Of Fate about him, till his quest
Brought him within unlikely hands,
   And saw the old Faith's young Defender
   Harnest in Luther's rebel bands.

Wolsey. A priest he had for mischief-mender,   190
   To justify his tyrant's work,
A priest who on foundation slender
Built himself Cardinal of York,
   And feasted high ; yet lookt for higher
   Employment for his knife and fork.   195
Lo ! on the brink of his desire,
   With one foot in the gates of Rome,
   Back he must come, on shameful hire,
To serve his master's turn at home,
1529.   And pack a Parliament to show   200
   A parting of the ways was come.
"The Pope denies me !   Let him go.
Henceforth in England shall be none."
   The Parliament in puppet-row
Jigg'd to that sounding tune set on,   205
   And crying "Out upon the Pope !"
   Contriv'd King Henry should be one.
1534.   Head of the Church ! Alas, the scope
   Of that great place involved no saint,

But very man coil'd up in rope   210
Of his own fleshly argument !
   Little knew Hodge of kings' high needs,
   But with kings' itch was soon acquaint.
When Catherine pines and Boleyn bleeds,
   And Cardinal York gives up two crosses   215
   To take that one which he who leads
Apes down to Hell deserves—these losses
   Glare mockery on the homely text
   Whereof Saint Use has scored the glosses
Observ'd by Hodge.   Hodge is perplext   220
   By scorn of good Queen Catherine.
   She is the King's wife, and this next
Shall be for him the Concubine.
   Is our hot King a wanton's lover ?
   It matters little.   She is fine,   225
Madness lies in the kissing of her,
   And she may get the Crown an heir ;
   Therefore let statesmanship discover
The way to bed—and put her there.
   But see now what ensues : the check   230
   Of Cardinal York and his affair ;
The King a Pope, and Boleyn's neck
   To expiate her womb's disaster ;
   But more, the Abbeys go to wreck.

*The
Monks
Depart.* The King is hot, the pace grows faster :   235
   Go your ways, Abbot, go your ways !

For Hodge 'tis but a change of master ;
For you, you've had your golden days.
  He sees you go without a sigh,
  Giving you neither blame nor praise :   240
Not after you need he outcry,
  For you were lord and he was lout ;
  And he had other fish to fry.
For when you put your broad lands out
  To who would yield you highest profit,   245
  You put your lordliness in doubt
And laid it in his mind to scoff it,
  Who must pay him to whom you had sold
  And get no groatsworth vantage of it,
Save a new lord besides an old.   250
  You and your times were out of joint,
  My Abbot ; zeal was more than cold ;
Your habit serv'd not to anoint,
  Your monk was little but a hood,
  And underneath a dog—at point.   255
Away with Gracedieu, Holy Rood,
  Champfleurs, Val Crucis, names like balms
  Wherewith some man adorn'd his God
As one would do himself an alms
  By hanging fond words on his dear—   260
  A fallen God can cause no qualms :
Adone with such unthrifty gear !
  Like martyr'd men with lidless eyes,
  Roofless, unglaz'd, the great shrines peer,

THE DESPOTS

Asking vain questions of the skies—   265
  Here is no room for such as ye;
  He who spreads not the truth spreads lies.
Go your ways, Glaston, Shaftesbury,
  Croyland and Jervaulx, Walsinghame;   269
  Let Christ Church help God's House to dree,
Shades of a shadow and a name!
  But watch you how the pointer swings
  And turns upon the shamer shame,
Who from the welter of new things
  Spewed out the pallium of the Pope,   275
  And cut the buttresses of kings.
Lo, for a knock to those who grope
  Unjustified by sacring oils!
  The climber strangled in his rope,
The robber snar'd in his own toils—   280
  Lo, what Time's whirligig shall bring!
  He sackt the Monks and sold their spoils
To who would dance as he should sing;
  And dance they did, to such a tone
  That they anon could sack the king.   285
Mourn not the Monks. Their day was done.
  Milestones upon a Roman road,
  They mark how far the pilgrim's gone,
And more, how far he still must plod:
  But here's a work at which Hodge winces, 290
  A work that robs him of his God.
Reforma- When Cromwell dipt in murder-rinses,
tion.

119

Less happy than his Polar Star,
Lost his head and saved his Prince his,
And quit the land he helpt to mar,   295
    He reiv'd the Church's body, and left
    Her soul alive for Henry's war.
Thus came the despot's crowning theft
    (Despot or Fly upon a Wheel);
    Penn'd like an adder in a cleft,   300
He flasht his fork, who felt the steel;
    And turning all ways in his pother,
    Girding, his torment to anneal,
Struck sideways at the Virgin Mother
    And the mild burden of her breast;   305
    And stole one God, and made no other.
Gone now the mercies of that nest
    Of purity without a smirch,
    All that men know of holiest
Aflower within a woman's curch: 310
    Now Doom fall heavy on the wretch
    Who turn'd Madonna out of church!
And it did fall.   His evil letch
    Found nothing good to serve it long.
    One woman stay'd him out to fetch   315
A son, and he died rotten and young;
    And of his girls, the one was gaunt
    With woman-sickness and wrought wrong;
The other, the great Termagant,
    Ate up her days, to man forbid,   320

THE DESPOTS

And left dry sticks, for fools to plant.
To sum the tale of all he did,
This bloat destroyer of his own
And other men's, ere we were rid
Of him, and like a bladder blown   325
By poisonous vapours seething in't
He broke and dropt, to stifle or drown—
Let these things be set fast in print :
First, having had our money's worth,
He laid hands on the coin in mint,   330
And thinn'd it ere he sent it forth
To tell the merchants of the South
What faith he kept up in the North ;
Next, having serv'd one God in youth,
He kept the badge too cheaply bought,   335
And prov'd himself from his own mouth
Defender of a thing of nought—
Nay, if like man the Master is,
His sacre is not worth a thought !
And last of his self-robberies   340
Ere to his unwept grave he gat :
He made the Estate which saddled his ;
Then died, clogg'd up with boils and fat.
Eater of women, thankless thief,
We never serv'd a worse than that.   345

*Eliza-
beth.*

Leave we the boy whose hour was brief :
Geneva only craved his breath ;

121

THE SONG OF THE PLOW

Leave blackbrow'd Mary to her grief,
Who serv'd the Lord of Life with death ;
 And hail the Queen of dauntless pluck   350
 The termagant Elizabeth !
Berufft, bering'd, befrizz'd, bestuck,
 You think, A doll ! unless you watch
 The wary eye coursing for luck,
If by good hap she make a catch   355
 And have you by the heartstring fast,
 Her prey, to stroke, and then to scratch.
O whim incarnate, iron cast
 In minion-texture filmy-frail !
 O falsely true, Queen first and last,   360
You tyrant fiery-soul'd, all hail !
 You stood for England, lookt no higher
 Than your own proven triple mail.
Mistress of wile and flaming ire,
 Wielding your passions for your turn ;   365
 Cozener and gamester, hardy liar,
Even now we come to you to learn
 What it needs face the world in arms
 If England's honour we would earn.

Hodge and the times. Hodge knew you not, nor guess'd the alarms   370
 That flew about your island hold ;
 He had his griefs for his own harms,
Left to the penury and cold
 Of lessening wages, stinted room,
 Strange gods—a sheep in alien fold   375

122

THE DESPOTS

Watcht by strange sheepdogs in the gloom.
  Sheepdogs or wolves ?   By what ambages
  They baffled you, you spoke the doom
Of Hodge, poor hireling of the ages,
  When Justices o' the Peace were set   380
  To rule the rate of his day's wages.
You say, He was free his work to let :
  Nay, he is free who rules the roost.
  My lord had Hodge within his net,
Since wages rule as victuals cost :   385
  All Hodge's freedom is to end
  His days, by giving up the ghost.
Nor could he hope his case to mend
  By asking comfort from the sky ;
  For you denied his constant friend,   390
The Mother with her Babe held high :
  He dared not hear his priest at Mass
  Teach him, *Thy God is standing nigh.*
He saw his friends and neighbours pass
  Broken and weeping by the way ;   395
  He said, These men were as I was,
And I must soon be even as they.
  Where are my saints who had my love ?
  And who will teach me how to pray ?
His betters might do well enough :   400
  They had the seas, they held the day—
  To trade with Boris Godounov
And come back to an English May,

123

And have the scent o' the hawthorn bush
　Borne by the West wind o'er the spray ;　405
And hear again an English thrush
　Flute the quiet hopefulness of life,
　Steadfast and high as a girl's blush
When she's a newly promist wife !
　Not this for him ; nor yet to find　410
　In tavern'd ease his bourn of strife,
Telling of Muscovy or Ind,
　Or of Benin the dangerous shore,
　Or of the blessed Trading wind.
Those men of yours were England's core,　415
　Your Drake and Martin Frobisher,
　Your Grenvilles, Davises and more,
Your Raleigh, pirate, courtier,
　Who brought Hodge home his weed and root,
　And lives while English blood's astir.　420
Hodge had no more of the golden loot ;
　And all he knew of your affrights
　Was when at work with heavy foot
He saw the beacons blaze the heights,
　To warn you Philip had set out　425
　For roaring days and stormy nights.

Hodge
and the
Poets.

Let Spenser sing of Colin Clout,
　And fill his book half full of hopes
　And half of grave Platonic doubt
To o'er-sophisticate his tropes　430

Which make you Queen of Faerie,
  While beerful Ben at Mermaid gropes
To write his way through pedantry—
  Hodge knew them not, nor was beknown
  Of them ;   but here's a certainty :   435
There mused a man in Stratford town
  To whom the wide world was an inn ;
  And there he sat, too wise to frown,
And watcht the folk go out and in ;
  And *he* knew Hodge, and how much ruth   440
  There lay behind Feste's flickering grin.
It raineth every day, in truth,
  Yet heart to meet it never fails ;
  And Hodge had still his merry tooth
For Mayings, high days and Wassails,   445
  For Christmas logs, Midsummer fires,
  For mummings, Waits and Winters' Tales.
Not his the sad heart that soon tires ;
  Saint Use hath still an antidote
  Against the hour, and still requires   450
Attendance at Court Halimote,
  View of Frankpledge, Assise of Ale ;
  And still he follows as by rote
His husbandry, and pays his gale
  For commonage.   Not yet is looming   455
  The hateful badge of those who fail,
The dreaded end—but that is coming.
  The black fog is not on his soul,

But as at sea you hear the booming
Foretell its gathering masses roll,   460
  So there are signs, if he were read,
  That the Poor House must be his goal.

1603. No more.   The goodly years are sped,
  The gallant heart is snapt in twain ;
  Flaming Elizabeth is dead,   465
Who reared a race to outrace Spain.
  They say she had no God, and truly—
  Only herself herself spoke plain ;
They say she had no heart, unduly—
  England had that and knew it bleed.   470
  Ruler of men, herself unruly,
She school'd herself to meet her need.
  Denied her sex, she play'd her part
  And held all England for her seed.
Queen after Curtmantle's own heart,   475
  Sleep well !   We scan our kings in vain
  For such another on the chart.

BOOK VIII

THE FALL OF THE KINGS

BOOK VIII : THE FALL OF THE KINGS

NOW for a hundred years I tread
  The embattled ways of strife and
   blame,
While you, Hodge, are as good as dead
For all you enter in the game :
 A hundred years' arbitrament   5
 By sword and clamour add their shame
To them who having you in pent
 Leave you acast like a kickt stone,
 While doited kings 'gainst Parliament
Shatter themselves and are undone.   10
 Whichever way the victory tends
 It matters not ; you profit none.
Your Gods are gone, your ghostly friends,
 Your saints flung out, your altars broke,
 Your housel scouted ; no amends   15
For you within the Holy Book,
 Nor is to be this many a year.
 Your old Church homely comfort spoke,
But where's your comfort in this gear
 Of Presbyters and Preaching Days ?   20

THE SONG OF THE PLOW

What get you from the pulpiteer,
Gaping to gather what he says ?
   The battle raves ; and as of yore
   You swinkt while knights rode their forays,
So now you bend your back to store   25
   The grain, or sow anew, or beat
   It out upon the threshing floor.
Not of the measure that you mete
   Shall it be meted you again :
   You work that gentlemen may eat,   30
They'll make your labouring in vain ;
   You go to plow that men may live,
   They go to battle who's to reign,
And whose the high prerogative.
   To you, good friend, it matters not   35
   Which gate it goes.   None has to give
A thought your way.   In the upshot
   You will be slave again, you'll find,
   When stale with strife the victors rot,
And get a blind king for the blind,   40
   To run corruption's dearest rigg
   And make corrupt all humankind.
Your county member, that staunch Whig,
   Will cry his sufferings for his views ;
   Some portly burgess from his gig   45
Vow you the King's downfall good news :
   The King was less your foe, God bless you,
   Than any tyrant you could choose !

THE FALL OF THE KINGS

He was least likely to oppress you
  By his remoteness of degree ;   50
  The men whose need is to possess you
Will make you fast once they are free
  To run without their leading strings.
  When the King's tied, so you will be.

The Four If kings must be, I'd have bad kings,   55
Stuarts.   For finally men turn and rend them ;
  Yet four ropeworthies clapt their wings
Before we had the grace to send them
  To join their kinsmen in the grave,   59
  With what support romance could lend them.
Four Stuarts : the one more fool than knave ;
  One drawn to knavery by his folly ;
  And one who bound himself a slave
To beastliness, lest melancholy
  Drave him to madness and despair ;   65
  And one given up to madness wholly,
Who sought to quicken the dead with air,
  And rather earn'd our scorn than hate.
James I.   You, who brought on us all this care,
Son of that pale mischance of Fate
  Of scarlet mouth and sidelong eyes,
  The lovelorn Daughter of Debate—
How were you furnisht for the Assize
  Whereto you needs must go to clean
  Your foolish head aburst with lies ?
                                                                 75

131

Perverse adventure ! Had you been
  Dominie in some village school,
  To fondle boys, or help them glean
The *Ut*-with-the-subjunctive rule ;
  And after such complacent labours   80
  To spend your evenings getting full
Of usquebaugh and shrilling havers
  Anent mankind's predestination,
  Election and such godly favours—
Had Fate so ruled, your generation   85
  Had not seen blood upon the Crown,
  Nor your son's son humiliation !
But you must needs hale kingship down
  With you the slippery ruinous steep ;
  It was for you, half wit, half clown,   90
Bemus'd by half-got scholarship,
  To lure your Order on to edge
  The sheer cliff hanging o'er the deep.
You craved the Tudor privilege ;
  But one, it seems, may steal a horse,   95
  T'other not look across the hedge.
The Houses now were learn'd in force,
  And knew to meet it with their own ;
  You drifted on from ill to worse,
Learning the less as you were known   100
  The better—Dotard, could I reach
  With ash-plant in my hand well-grown
The round of your unholy breech,

THE FALL OF THE KINGS

Unto your headpiece wryly jointed
There were a lesson good to teach   105
To him who boasts him Lord's Anointed !
By falsehood's shelving whirlpool way

To learn this truth was Charles appointed,
That kings, like dogs, will have their day ;
And when the Commons lockt the door   110

In spite of him, and said their say,
They wrote great names upon the score.
Their say was said, and more by token,
They wrote it plain for him to pore ;
They made that true, not truly spoken :   115
Henceforth no king should go to break
Their House, and not himself be broken.

Seven years it was ere they could make
That writing true ; but each red word
Was written deep, each word a wake   120
That followed on the furrowing sword :
Seven years of riot and ill heat,
Until the rout on Naseby sward
Brought Charles's head to Cromwell's feet
He had been happier to foresee   125
Ere he began that he was beat.

And what of Hodge, and where stood he
Between Prince Rupert and Prince Pym ?
A Tweedledum and Tweedledee

133

Such transient monarchs were to him.   130
   Indifferently their armies ranged,
   Indifferent claim'd his life and limb
For their affair : he was estranged
   From both of them and their disasters,
   And in the event he stood exchanged   135
From one to some five hundred masters.
   Betwixt King Cromwell and King Charles,
   Betwixt old priests and new-fledg'd pastors
There's little difference to poor carles,
   Plying the harrow and the hoe   140
   On fields as guiltless of their snarls.
What of Election can he know
   Or should he know, who has no choice ;
   Or Grand Remonstrance, whether or no—
The patient plodder without voice ?   145
   Silent, he judges this at least,
   Having no share in such annoys,
Presbyter's but longwritten Priest,
   And any shackle serves to lame
   The soul of man or leg of beast.   150
As for the Lord, He stands the same
   Tho' church become a steeple-house,
   And he be given a Hebrew name
Which Praise-God Barebones thunderous
   Hinges upon the Jews' dark story,   155
   Beating the pulpit-ledge to rouse
His flock to dangers minatory—

While at his feet in graven brass
Dom Galfrid smiles, expecting glory !
Hodge, like a rock, sees all this pass   160
  As rain, wind-driven in a sheet,
  Whereto he turns, as doth the ass,
His rounded back, and lets it beat
  About his ears.   The winds blow high,
  The dense cloud-masses pack and meet,   165
Or ragged banners part and fly
  Eager and low down—still the rents
  Reveal the blue robe of the sky.

1469, January.
Strange news shrills o'er the winter bents,
  Over the waters of the Plain,   170
  Over the downs to shepherds' tents :
" Have ye not heard ?   The King is slain.
  They do report him man of sin,
  They say no king shall come again :
But what say you ?   If they begin   175
  With king, where shall they end ?   For sure,
  When a king goes, a king comes in."

Cromwell and his Kind.
A king indeed was come, to cure
  By purge the Commons, too much tied
  To precedent.   He took the pow'r   180
He had destroy'd as regicide ;
  And found one thing to bit the horse,
  But quite another thing to ride.
In England now surg'd up a force

135

Slow-gather'd thro' the centuries,   185
Which like a headed watercourse
That burst the dam, swept tyrannies—
All tyrannies except its own—
Rolling and rocking to their knees.

The Middle Class.

Within the dense and hiving town,   190
  Within the thronging street and mart
  This power was gender'd, which had grown
Unwatcht and hid in England's heart.
  Long-pondering, of heavy foot,
  Not mov'd by words, not heeding art,   195
Taking its good and holding to't
  Thro' times of heat and times of cold,
  Like our great oaks it struck its root
Deep in the very fund of the mould,
  So deep that no man should be got   200
  Henceforth and not hold as it hold.
Plain men and just are these, not hot
  Nor cold, but funded in the mean ;
  Their gods are God, others are not ;
Only thro' their eyes is truth seen :   205
  Strangers have dealing fair, withal
  They doubt a foreigner can be clean.
Here was the people in whose thrall
  Hodge and his kind must come to stand,
  Hodge the poor aboriginal   210
Who serv'd, because he was, the land,

Harbour'd as well as labourer,
Who in her bosom dar'd his hand.
But as the Norman conqueror
    Engrafted on our English stem   215
    His pride of place and his honour,
So showed these panoplies in them
    Who left the ranks of their array
    And claim'd the master's diadem.
More Norman than the Normans they,   220
    With more of pride, and less of care
    To flush with honour their cold clay,
They rode Hodge down and left him there,
    Gaunt as the face of weather'd rock,
    Enserf'd again, in the old despair.   225
There fell a hush upon the folk
    Such as at folding down of night
    Silences suddenly the flock ;
Or as when all the world is white
    With new-faln snow, the wagon's creak   230
    Sounds faint, as if the load was light
Upon the Earth, who car'd not speak—
    So Englishmen their labours took,
    And made a Sabbath all the week.
That was the Sabbath of the Book,   235
    Connoted by the Pharisees.
    If they teach truly we may look
For an eternity of these.

THE SONG OF THE PLOW

Now sooth it is, each temporal mood
Is to itself its own disease,   240
And with what zeal we win our good
With just so much we next abhor it,
And turn to long-rejected food,
And vow ourselves the better for it—
So England, sicken'd of her new,   245
, Cried up her old throne, to restore it.
The Wastrel comes, of sallow hue,
The Medicean effigy
Stampt on a heart as fond, untrue
And vile as even a Stuart's can be ;   250
The man who laughs, lest in some glass
His own despair he chance to see
And shriek his own disgustfulness.
Now we are jigging in a dance
Which stays not while the death-carts pass ; 255
Now we get hire and whores from France
And bless the given to the giver ;
Now we find perils to enhance
Our feasts—the Dutchmen in the river ;
And Master Pepys, at grips with life,   260
Recording triumphs of the liver.
While Master Pepys with Bagwell's wife
Does Bagwell wrong on Deptford hard,
And whoredom and the Plague, both rife,
Promise corruption for reward,   265
Whom shall we teach, of all on hire,

138

To break the box of spikenard
And find in honesty new desire ?
  Signs of the times were writ in red,
  The streaming pennons of the Fire ;   270
Yet to our buzzards overfed
  Virtue was Pandarus to Vice ;
  A maiden was a maidenhead,
A maidenhead a matter of price :
  When everything was out for sale,   275
  Small wonder Hodge was merchandise.

He was the first goods tied in bale,
  No sooner were the three Estates,
  Kings, Lords, and Landlords, fresh and hale
Upon their thrones, behind their gates.   280
  England, rejoice ! Your griefs are laid ;
  Now feast, while they attend the Fates.
Your King is home, be not afraid :
  Here are the Lords and faithful Commons
  Fathers of many nations made,   285
As saith the Epistle to the Romans,
  Now all agog to justify
  What they assume to be a summons.
They took first charge of husbandry,
  And lest Hodge might get out of hand   290
  Or, seeking work, stray large and by,
Tied him securely to the land :
  No poor man now should leave his vill

*Hodge
bound
again,
1662.*

But could be sent back on demand.
Would you know why ?   The village till   295
    Was answerable for its poor ;
    But if those rascals roam'd at will,
Who was to know what Poorhouse door
    They might not batter with their quest
    For victual or night's furniture ?   300
A wandering peasantry's a pest ;
    But we'll have no cast-iron hedges ;
    Whither the scamp goes let him rest,
On giving " reasonable pledges."
    Nay, even more, such our possession   305
    Of care for all men's privileges,
Hodge shall have leave his suit to press on
    From Court to Court, and take his plea
    From Petty unto Quarter Session,
From two landlords to twenty-three.   310
    Distracted once, now happy Nation !
    All things are as they us'd to be,
All men in the old concatenation,
    The King enthron'd and Hodge enthrall'd :
    Here is indeed a Restoration,   315
The which, if peace it may be call'd,
    Which is a silence like a tomb's,
    Will keep the fortunate install'd
Within their handsome dining-rooms,
    Keeping domestic festival,   320
    Ruling the nation with their dooms,

BOOK IX: STRONG DELIVERER

WHEN winds are high and lands adust,
 And day no longer than the night,
 When grass-spears dimple the earth's
  crust,
Pricking the glebe with points of light—
 High in new Heaven shrills the lark, 5
 Scattering his fount of song in flight;
There is a burnish on bole and bark,
 A bloom upon the woodland sere ;
 The dark yews wear a glossier dark,
Blue fire illumes the juniper : 10
 Earth robes herself in golden moss,
 The birthday mantle of the year !
The years pursue, gain after loss,
 And fleeting after them this Rime,
 Like the great river Okeanos, 15
Must gird the globe in space and time.
 Faster or slower, clear or dense
 As vision grants, gross or sublime,
The running verse engulfs the sense
 And laps it onward, free and brave 20
 As following years. Quick and intense

*ars
d this
me.

145   L

THE SONG OF THE PLOW

One line swims from another's grave,
   Surging, until the backwash holds it,
   And the last rime comes like a wave,
Spent in the new thought that enfolds it.   25
   So is it with our round of days :
   The womb, conceiving new life, moulds it
Deeply with runes of the ancient ways
   Wherein itself was deeply prest.
   Forth to strange airs and new forays   30
Come we, with memories of the nest ;
   And so the Life-Sap surges on
   Perennial through woman's breast.
The new, afore the old is gone,
   Is reinforced by backward ebb,   35
   And towering, crashes on the stone
And is flung back, a criss-cross web
   Of broken waves, to find a home
   In the new-gathering, curving neb
Of sliding water cream'd with foam.   40

The New Read there a figure of the truth
in the   The insurgents learn'd who broke with Rome,
Old. When despot Henry slak'd his tooth
   In robbery, and the deed was done
   Which reft our English of the sooth   45
Lore of the Virgin and her Son.
   They broke the Church, but of the old
   Splinters and sherds another one

The breakers built, a shapelier fold.
   A brick from here, a tile from there,   50
   Foundations of the antick mould ;
Snugly within, the Bishop's chair,
   And that blest thing, a liturgy
   Marking the limits to a hair
Of what your trade with God should be,   55
   Of when you stood and when you sat,
   Of apathy and ecstasy.
Μηδὲν ἄγαν, the saw comes pat ;
   They rear'd a fabric all to please,
   Secure from heat—and rather flat.   60
O finely temper'd balances
   Between the old priests and the newer,
   What shall the simple do with these,
Your plowman, hodman, drawer, hewer ?
   He seeks assurance that his call   65
   Out of the deep His aid procure
Who made and watcht and bled for all,
   Who was a well-spring in the heat,
   Who heedeth how the sparrows fall—
You give him Articles for his meat,   70
   A gruel of logic for his fountain
   Of grace, and bid him drink of it !

Old
he
v.   When George Fox, musing on his mountain,
    Turn'd his rapt eyes adown the steep,
    He saw the peoples packt past counting,   75

Straying in herds like driven sheep,
　With open mouths and blacken'd tongues,
　Too dust-begone and dry to weep ;
So vow'd himself to right their wrongs
　And labour'd all his nights and days,　　80
　Pointing his periods with rude songs
All of his secret inner rays
　Of light divine ; and whom he brought
　Into his quiet reflective ways
Of soberness, put sober thought　　85
　In their sons' sons, though few they be.
　In a white light was Bunyan caught,
Which curb'd him sharply in his glee,
　Blazing before his alter'd face
　Blank horror of eternity.　　90
Less dar'd he think of God's free grace
　Than of the dreadful wrath to come ;
　Less could he heed the sick man's case
For thinking of his endless doom.
　He cried the worm, the burning coals,　　95
　The fog, the groaning and the gloom ;
And vain his thunderous warning rolls
　Over men bound in hunger-stress,
　Who never knew that they had souls,
So keen their bodies' wretchedness.　　100
　But now,—as when old misery
　Held Hodge in bondage remediless,
And the Gray Men from oversea

Brought gentle deed and honest word
To teach him what his hope might be 105
If a poor Maid could bear our Lord,
And a poor Child be God indeed
(Which was the work of Bonaccord,
Sowing in England Francis' seed,
Whereof the comfort has been ours 110
Thro' many a year of dearth and need)—
Now, when that failed us, and dark hours
Came back, with none to lead us higher,
For Francis' faith that broke in flowers

sley. Came Wesley's, ministering with fire. 115
O Strong Deliverer, with reprieve
For all who heard your heart suspire !

8. When on that Pentecostal Eve
You stood beside your brother's bed
And testified, saying, I believe, 120
Were not the Tongues about your head ?
When your apostolate began
Was there no rising from the dead ?

*e
ild a
an.* Francis proclaim'd a Child that ran
And shelter'd in His Mother's lap ;— 125
But now the Child was full-grown Man
With no more need to seek the pap,
Ready His Father's business
To be about, with sight mayhap
Of that last Cup of bitterness 130

Which He must drink, and of another
Hereafter to be pour'd.   No less
Did Wesley, when Christ and His Mother
Were turn'd away, and He unknown,
Than bring Him back to be our Brother,   135
Than bring Him back a Man full-grown,
To take our burden up and bear it
Until each man could lift his own.
Says he, All need grace, all can share it,
All men may know its birth assured;   140
Having it, each man shall declare it,
That all be holiness in the Lord.
By these five signs the saint's betray'd,
As there are five needs to a sword—
Hilt, guard and point and two-edg'd blade.   145
These doctrines Wesley liv'd to prove,
And died, and knew himself apaid.
For as one new caught-up in love
Feels a great peace with all the world,
And thinks himself the root thereof,   150
Whereas the truth is, he is engirl'd ;
And steept in tender thought of her,
Sees gentleness like dew empearl'd
On all gross nature, reading there
The quiet secrets of her heart—   155
So Hodge, with Christ-love all astir,

Hodge and the Doctrine. Trudg'd housell'd by his horse and cart,
Ignorant sacramentalist,

Inspir'd to do his daily part
With Christ in him and him in Christ.   160
   Afield, at home, a new-heard voice
   Bids him be sure.   As if new-kiss'd
He sees his faded wife ; his boys
   And girls shine with reflected grace
   Of his new holiness ; new joys   165
Redeem his fetid dwelling-place—
   The beaten floor, the bed of leaves
   Where they must huddle and make no case
Of the rat busy in the eaves.
   Let all these be what bait they can   170
   For Parliament, that den of thieves,
To fasten on ; in his new plan
   He holds by Christ the Crucified,
   Who found him serf and left him man.

The High What matter though Sir Robert ride   175
World.   The sot in ermine, and rule out
   All factions but his own ?   His pride
Is of earth earthy ; let him grout
   With heavy wantons in a stye,
   And politicians ring his snout !   180
Our commerce now is with the sky ;
   The news is that Christ died for men,
   And is here yet, and now is nigh.
So Hodge transcended his poor den   184
   Whilst the first German kings learnt manners,

While his own sons were crimpt and then
Sent out to vex the Frenchmen's banners.
  Afoot, afloat, by sea and plain,
  From Finisterre to the Savannahs ;
At Fontenoy and Minden slain   190
  Or batter'd out of recollection,
  The press'd men serv'd their term of pain,
Unto the Devil choice refection ;
  And oversea left bleaching bones
  Expecting joyful resurrection.   195
So be't ! But Wesley's trumpet tones
  Made men, where had been herded cattle,
  Heedless as well of ribald stones
As of the shock of Rodney's battle.
  The world, the flesh, the devil beat   200
  Against them and approv'd their mettle ;
For they had been given a ghostly meat
  Wherewith to face what ills betided,
  Though they had little else to eat.
And the high world (while Hodge abided) 205
  Hunted its pleasures, diced and play'd ;
  The Gunnings took the air, provided
With footguards for their Park parade ;
  Chesterfield sneers, the Doctor winces,
  Horace affects the masquerade :   210
Which Opera serve you, King's or Prince's ?
  Are you for pistols or for swords ?
  Has Q. his mistress ? Who Selwyn's is ?

STRONG DELIVERER

Goes Pulteney to the House of Lords ?
And in the fields whence these high noddies 215
   Drain nutriment, women in hordes,
Stone-picking, tossing dung, their bodies
   Marr'd by the weather, with the stains
   Of loam and sweat on smock or bodice,
Work thro' the sunshine and the rains ;   220
   And men are there with fierce bright eyes,
   And children, scar'd by hunger-pains
To snatch like young wolves, make a prize
   Of a bird-bitten turnip cast
   Beside a furrow, thick with flies.   225
No tramp of men: silence is vast
   Upon the country ; but in town
   The weavers fight to break their fast,
And the dragoons must ride them down.
   Horace from cloistral Berkeley Square,   230
   His shapely brow pucker'd to frown,
Walks out to see the houses flare,
   And shrewdly reads within the fog
   More than a Riot Act affair.
King Stork is minister to King Log,   235
   Says he, and ponders much the end,
   Tying a ribbon for his dog,
Or couplet for his lady friend.
   The case was worse than he conceiv'd—
   He saw, but had no care to mend—   240
But better in that one man liv'd

153

To give them of the best he had,
To know in Whom they had believ'd :
John Wesley on his ambling pad,
   With comfort for them in his pocket,   245
   Keeping the road, patient and glad
To serve their emptiness and stock it.
   His work was done ere he was dead,
   Like a spent candle in the socket.
Burning his life down to a shred,   250
   And spearing up with his last breath
   Into a flame unmeasurèd
But by the darkness after death.

BOOK X

THE LAST THEFT

BOOK X : THE LAST THEFT

*Block-
heads'
Rule.*

WHEN North was rooted for our woes,
    And Sackville taught the American
    How English landlords would dispose
Of him, as neither God nor man
    Nor devil might with Englishry   5
    Once free, the last great theft began ;
For being shut of robbery
    Abroad, they lookt at home, to pull
    Breast-feathers from the smaller fry
To make their nests more comfortable.   10

*George
III.*

    Apt leader you, O George the Third,
    Pious and obstinate, proud and dull,
To cushion like a nesting bird
    On your fleeced subjects, and to prate
    With wagging head and stammer'd word   15
Of England happy, free and great,
    With lords in parks beneficent,
    And peasants beaming—on the estate.
All's well : the farmer pays the rent,
    The labourer's worthy of his hire ;   20
    My lords are in the Parliament,

And God, like a reposeful squire,
  Hears Cherubim and Seraphim
  Sing Order to the tuneful lyre ;
Wonderful order, made by Him   25
  For angels and subservient nations,
  Whereby alone His world goes trim
When all men keep their proper stations :
  The highly placed, in their high places,
  The lowly serving them—on rations.   30
Excellent world ! but for such races
  As Boston breeds for Bunker Hill,
  Or France, encumber'd with disgraces
Of the poor, who choose not to lie still,
  But break the bonds which Fates decree   35
  And grind their lords in their own mill.
From men's high courage to be free,
  From Washington and Lafayette
  You nothing learn'd.   Hot butchery
Of men wrought frantic left you yet   40
  Bemus'd with pride, the sort that clings
  To dulness, lest hope or regret
Should move it.   To your whip of stings
  You added scorpions.   White and blind,
  You scor'd your reign with gibbet-swings.   45
You were well serv'd.   After your kind,
  Bute, Grafton, North, high-sniffing sires,
  Like towering falcons take the wind
In pride of place.   The mob admires,

Till Johnny Wilkes or Gordon kindles   50
  Them liberal or protestant fires ;
And then their admiration dwindles.
  But there's to deal with sterner stuff
  Which the Blind Women at their spindles
Are twisting for you.   Soon enough   55
  You'll find your destinies on earth,
  With Europe handled by the scruff.

rogress
d the
ountry-
an.

All's well, say you ?   But there's this dearth,
  A double dearth which needs contriving ;
  The great need money for their mirth,   60
The towns need bread where swarms are hiving,
  And beer—O find us malt for brewing !
  Sad that the measure of their thriving
Should be the countryman's undoing,
  But so it was.   When Arthur Young,   65
  Concern'd with economic ruin,
Cried up the properties of dung
  Which in hedg'd land your yield quadruples,
  He serv'd the gamester and the bung,
And had no lack of ardent pupils.   70
  The Open Lands must go, all said ;
  This was no age for reverent scruples ;
Saint Use-and-Wont was dying or dead—
  Bury him deep, and let us have
  Utility for saint instead.   75
The lawyers dig his handsome grave ;

His epitaph in Private Bills
Is courtly writ.   Indifferent brave
It sounds : WHEREAS, for all our ills
A remedy lies close to hand,   80
Now therefore WE redeem the hills
And valleys of all champion land.
To that effect !   The Muse abridges
All that you need not understand.
Keep watchful eye for grassy ridges   85
When next upon your country walk,
Which run their course thro' dykes and hedges:
Dead husbandry of furrow and balk,
Telling of Hodge's life bypast
When his own ox-plow turn'd the chalk,   90
And from his own land he broke fast.

The Old   Before the days of sword and helm,
Village.   Before the Norman bolt was cast,
The village lay, a little realm,
The Manor with its three estates ;   95
About it, robed in oak and elm,
The lord's demesne, with pale and gates.
Within was justice done for all,
The courts were held, the runagates
Corrected ; but beyond the hall   100
And its demesne lay the lord's wood,
Wherein the tenants at the fall
Might turn their pigs to rout for food—

There they might gather up the drift,
  Or cut of bracken what they would.　　　105
At the wood's edge the commons lift
  Towards the sky their flame of gorse ;
  There without charter or lord's gift
Each cottager might feed his horse,
  His cow and calf, his sheep and pig,　　110
  By ancient custom which had force
Of law behind it.　Some might dig
  For marl or gravel, or some cut
  Peat for their firing.　Little and big,
All fared alike ; and one was put　　　115
  For overseer of waste and copse,
  That no man's right another's shut.
The roundsman guarded growing crops,
  The herd kept watch upon the hurst ;
  Sharp over all the Reeve's eye drops.　　120
The tilth lay open, strips disperst,
  Sever'd by balks, roodland from roodland ;
  All turn'd by lot, best with the worst ;
You might have all your shots of good land,
  Or might have none—but all the land　　125
  Was open fallow, like the woodland,
Like common pastures, no beast bann'd,
  Save geese, whose droppings are a poison,
  When once the fields were glean'd by hand.
So, after men, the beasts had foison ;　　130
  And it stayed fallow for a mowing,

While the next field had men and boys on
To plow against the winter's sowing.
  Two course or three, so custom fared,
  With grass and corn alternate growing.   135
Here, strip and strip, all manner shared,
  The lord, the parson, yeoman bold,
  The cottager, and he who had dared
Hoodwink the law of copyhold ;
  For even him the use took in   140
  If he had shelter from the cold.
There was no man too poor to win
  His own subsistence, or too haut
  To harvest with his lowlier kin :
All had their dues of boone and bote,   145
  Each had the judgment of his peers ;
  For in their Court of Halimote
The tenants were the justiciers ;
  The Frankpledge found the fault, and then
  The fine was laid about his ears   150
Who faulted, or a ruder pain.

*The New
Farming.*   So once all England stood, so yet
  Hodge had his status. With free men
He walkt free man, his only fret
  His own mishandling. Now all goes,   155
  And he must join the rueful set
Of them who fell as others rose ;
  For now, with need and common sense,

162

Covetousness cries out, Enclose !
The time was come for hedge and fence,   160
   That is most true.   But so is this,
   That you'll not profit of your pence
If they are got by *gormandise.*
   Hodge lays a robbery at your door
   When with your own land you took his.   165

eft. Two ways of ravishing the poor :
   The one to squeeze him in your fist ;
   T'other to tax his portion more
Than he can pay and still subsist.
   The second was the plan found good   170
   By your rural economist.
He dealt the lands out, tilth and wood,
   Pasture and common, right of soil :
   So much to the lord, to Hodge his rood
Or half-rood—God reward his toil !   175
   But stay : " Good man, 'tis yours, we pledge it
   A pightle fair to mend or spoil ;
Parva sed apta we allege it,
   And it is yours by stroke of pen—
   With this provision, that you hedge it."   180
dge " Hedge it !   But 'twill not feed my hen !
.   'Tis not enough to turn a pig in.
   And where shall I find money then
To buy me pales, or dung to dig in ?
   What shall I do, enclos'd, encas'd,   185
   One rood for beasts and us to lig in ?

163

THE SONG OF THE PLOW

I had my freedom of the waste,
  I took my share with my good neighbours ;
  There was enough for all to taste—
And I'm to sing on pipes and tabors   190
  The blessings of this new cockloft,
  And look to prosper by my labours ?
You tell me Parliament is soft
  To property ; but all I know
  Is this, I had land with my croft,   195
And now have none. I had a cow,
  And she's been sold for want of keep—
  Your Parliament got her I allow.
These thirty year I've kept your sheep ;
  I've serv'd you well for little gain ;   200
  I had my bit of land to reap,
I had my beast, or maybe twain.
  They kept me in milk or gave me meat ;
  I stood foursquare to wind and rain,
Free of my land, on my two feet—   205
  And who should know as well as you
  That a man's own bread is most sweet ? "

The End of Colin Clout. But no ! The Houses played the Jew—
  Beggar-my-neighbour or Odd-man-out—
  The land of many went to few,   210
And there was an end of Colin Clout.
  They held our English earth so dear
  That Englishmen must go without.

164

THE LAST THEFT

His Grace the Duke, that staunch Whig peer,
   Who held within his gates and lodge   215
   Three thousand acres for his deer,
Cast eyes upon the rood of Hodge.
   " What means this waste ? Enclose the moor!"
   And it was done, by lawyers' dodge.
The poor had less, the rich had more ;   220
   For a hundred years the game was play'd
   Out and about ; and when 'twas o'er
Scarce was a peasant had a spade
   With a lugg of land to use it on
   And earn his provand with the blade.   225
O earth made kindly by the sun,
   O land of tilth and pasture field,
   Where men have raised up men and won
By labour of your bountiful yield,
   What ghosts of wrong'd dead men oppress 230
   The sweet air blowing o'er the weald !
What hearts wrung dry in bitterness,
   What thews have husbanded in vain
   The mercy of your fruitfulness,
What tears have water'd in your grain !   235
   How shall a man have heart to rest
   On buried centuries of pain ?
Whither went they, the dispossest ?
   Some dar'd new life across the seas ;
   A many sank ; the swarming nest   240
Of town drew some to drug their knees

And dim their eyes in air that's not
Air, but the reek of lung-disease.
The crimps had some, the press-gang got
   Some, and the jail some; some were flung 245
   Into the galley-ship to rot
Or reach the land whence no man's tongue
   Could sound his misery worse than death
   (Death was their gain); and some were hung.
The rest adrift, like winter breath, 250
   Film'd the vision, and faded then,
   Serving Malthus his shibboleth,
That vice is good for mortal men—
   The smug philosopher theorizing
   The paupers hiving in their den. 255
There's this to approve his moralizing—
   When Hodge was elbow'd from the soil
   Five millions of him was the sizing:
Now some poor half a million toil.

1793.   The spendthrift century has run 260
   Its round of cozenage and spoil;
And now, my lords, a game's begun
   Which ought your credit to enhance,
   The year that sees Napoleon
On ragged wings stoop over France. 265
   Quick, turn your back on Speenhamlond,
   And find a use for Hodge perchance!
You fought your own, to make them bond,

Now here's a peril lest you fall
  Yourselves to servitude beyond   270
Any your mastership has at call.
  Rob Hodge no more, for here is risen
  A greater robber than you all.
Yet again, no ! The whip, the prison,
  The gibbet fatten. New offences   275
  Are made each day ; and each new treason
Leaves fewer men for your defences.
  You cannot learn that to be brute
  Makes him a brute, whose goaded senses
Drive him to put beyond dispute   280
  The wrong for which he jeopardizes,
  Whether or not he's driven to't.
And all the rest whom your Assizes
  Cannot avail to coop or cow,
  You drive to pauper's stock devices   285
Of cringing, whining, falling low
  To take your flung alms as from God,
  And curse you as they mop and mow.
Disastrous blockheads, with what rod
  You ruled withal, to you some day   290
  It shall be measur'd. With a nod
The great Assessor will look your way :
  " These fools, self-chosen, led the blind,
  And prov'd themselves blinder than they ;
For where else in the world d'you find   295
  Tillers kept off their land of tillage,

Save in this realm o' the South-West wind ? "
So I leave you, thieves of the village,
　To bring the land you went to mar
　Face to face with a greater pillage—　　300
Two-and-twenty years of war.

*Village
Twilight.*　Yet in the village you might muse
　Under the silver evening star :
The men, the houses, shrouded yews,
　The long church folding into the night　305
　Still in the holding of Saint Use
As in days when his shrine was bright.
　Still on his milestone, feeling the peace
　Of the level evening light,
His stick between his gnarly knees,　　310
　Gaffer sits in hempen smock
　With clear blue eyes for all he sees
'Neath craggy brows like weather'd rock :
　Small white houses about a green,
　Dust behind from a homing flock ;　　315
Ducks on the pond's edge nibble and preen
　Their necks ; in the great elm's heavy shade
　A dim couple, the king and queen
Of life-to-come, young man, young maid.
　Gaffer nods from the judgment-seat :　　320
　All these things have been sung or said
From the beginning ; first the sweet,
　Then the bitter.　We spend our days

As a tale that is told or writ.
Youth is tall, with a foolish face   325
  All hot flush and thoughts unskill'd,
  Who wears his jacket with high grace
Like a hussar, the sleeve not fill'd.
  His words are shy, his deeds are bolder ;
  He leans and presses. She is thrill'd.   330
She should be younger or else colder,
  That dreaming lass with neck of snow
  And curl astray upon her shoulder,
Who feels the colour burn and glow
  As answer to the question trips   335
  Why the young man should want her so.
My dear, come home, the world has whips
  For such as quit the apron-string ;
  And after kissing of the lips
The biting comes, the rue and sting.   340
  Come home : see what she thinks of you,
  The moon, half hid in a golden ring.

BOOK XI

WATERLOO AND PETERLOO

BOOK XI: WATERLOO AND PETERLOO

he
yrants'
ar.

L ET sing who will, on iron wires,
　　The twenty-two years' war ; let cry
　　Who will the guerdon of our sires
Who on the shot-swept *Victory*
　　Saw Nelson fall, or on the plain　　　　5
　　Where the Zadorra sluiced his dry
And gaping channel with red rain
　　Drave Marmont back the mountain road,
　　And left five thousand English slain ;
Or Waterloo, that field of blood,　　　　10
　　Where the great Robber found his peer,
　　And he who had trod the world saw trod
The legions of his last career :
　　Sing brazen-throated he who will
　　These crowning mercies !　I must veer　15
To dip my rustic-pointed quill
　　In drabber ink.　My ballad-scroll
　　Must voice the anguish deep and still
Of strife more bitter, where the toll
　　Was paid in heartbreak and despair,　　20
　　And men made war upon the soul.
Nelson. O Nelson, stepping debonair

173

THE SONG OF THE PLOW

The deck of death !   O wooden Duke,
  Scorner of them by whom you were
Serv'd hero, whose hard answer took   25
  A gibbet-shape to their acclaim,
  Not here for tribute shall you look !
Happier was Nelson, whose pure flame
  Spir'd upwards one short hour supreme,
  And flashing left no shade of blame   30
Upon a life spent like a dream,
  Intense in purpose, sheer and gay
  With love to light it, like a beam
Out of the West at shut of day.
  Happy who dies in utmost deed !   35
Welling-   But you, with head and name grown gray,
ton.   Must overlive the work you did
  Abroad, and come back home to do
  Vengeance on them whose crime was need :
We are to see you of that crew   40
  Who drove our English into riot.
  Peterloo follows Waterloo ;
We are to see your dream of quiet
  At Winchester be realiz'd,
  And victims of potato-diet,   45
Wretches by famine ill-advis'd,
  Strung up, or hounded from the land
  Which starv'd them mad, and then mainpris'd.
Seek nothing here but reprimand,
  O wooden Duke ! The men you drove   50

In Spain had little at your hand
But whip and spur to make them move.
   They serv'd you well, but neither they
   Nor theirs had call to owe you love.
Love is not won by battle-fray ;   55
   And as for honour, who would grudge
   Your Duchies or your Strathfieldsaye ?
Not I, nor any son of Hodge.
   Is there no braver work than war ?
   You who think lightly of the drudge,   60
Take thought of what he drudges for :
   Love of the land, the labour's sake,
   Love of a woman, and the store
Beneath her heart, of his own make !—
   Are these things nothing?   Heavy and dull, 65
   Can blood alone your gross heart slake ?
Must you put tiger up and bull
   To shame the dove? or see the mail'd
   Adventurer only purposeful ?
Then vainly Christ the Lord was nail'd,   70
   And King Apollo herding cattle
   With all his passion nought avail'd !
Have we no shame even yet to battle,
   Seeing how German wolves can wage it,
   Who seek in drum-tap and death-rattle   75
Balm for their itching, to assuage it ?
   What purpose our high hearts to tear
   If not to spend the beast, and cage it ?

THE SONG OF THE PLOW

1812,
26 Nov-
ember.

In eighteen-twelve, appointed year
    Which grip'd the Robber's heart in ice,   80
Hodge learn'd that victory costs as dear
As other martial merchandise,
    The beat no worse off than the stronger.
    When corn went up to famine price,
And starving weavers mad with hunger   85
    Brake looms because their bellies rav'd,
    What remedy had the victory-monger
But hanging—or what gained ?   He stav'd
    The harrowing of the proud awhile,
    And won the death-hush that he crav'd ;   90
Then when the King of Elba's isle
    Made himself Lord of Earth again,
    Needing whom he had held for vile,

1815,
18 June.

He harness'd them to his war-train.
    And they stood firm, in hollow blocks   95
    Of red upon the dripping plain,
While men and horses drave in shocks
    Of headlong battle, front and flanks,
    And brake like water on the rocks,
But never brake our English ranks.   100
    They made the man who had scorn'd them.
      Say,
    England, how did you give them thanks ?
By Sidmouth and by Castlereagh,
    Twin gods set up to scourge our vices,
    More ready to fear than we to pay !   105

16.   For down went corn and up went prices,
     And madden'd operatives for food
     Serried, and took their own devices,
  Since none else show'd them any good ;
     And English Justices of Peace   110
19.   Swam Peterloo in English blood.
Then found the Doctor remedies
     For men whose sickness was starvation,
     Six whips to down their failing knees,
  Six Acts to pin them to their station :   115
     What gat he from the hearts he broke
     And heads he bow'd but execration ?
He gain'd a silence, like a smoke
     Upon the earth, while the addle-head
     Of George the Third let slip the yoke   120
For sixty years unmerited.
     They changed a dullard for a rogue
20.   When a fourth George reign'd in his stead ;
Who made adultery the vogue
     At Court, and wail'd his griefs aloud   125
     When his wife swell'd the catalogue
Of them who seeded what he plow'd.
     After him raced the rout of shame,
     The lewd, the fond, the empty-proud—
Alvanley, Yarmouth, Jersey's dame,   130
     The Beau, the Poodle, in carouse,
     While England sicken'd at the game ;
And all the wit of Holland House,

All Bowood's talk and Woburn's treasure,
Spent not the value of a louse   135
On goaded men's content or pleasure.
  Such were your masters, England, while
  Hodge lay awaiting your high leisure ;
The vile defended by the vile,
  With Ellenborough to wield the sword   140
  Of Justice in the royal smile,
Aflame before the ragged horde
  Who dare pick food not grudg'd a bird,
  Or stint the franchise of their lord.
Life-sentence falls upon the herd   145
  Who gleans the woods for wife and child,
  Risking the man-trap, not deterr'd
By hanging judge, or mitred, mild
  Descendants of the Fisherman
  Who guard their pent sheep from the wild 150
By hanging stragglers all they can !

The
Reform-
ers.
Yet audible thro' those mute years
  A murmur'd music swell'd and ran ;
And there were men who scouted fears :
  Parson Tooke with his razor-wit,   155
  And Grey, the first among his peers,
And Cobbett with his centre-bit,
  That eye which saw a spade a spade
  However knaves might varnish it ;
Thelwall too, Cochrane, tough sea-blade,   160

178

Romilly and polite Burdett
Who, flaunting out the part he play'd,
Danced to the Tower in minuet ;
   Last, like a restless tocsin-bell,
   Mocking and brazen, resonant yet,   165
Byron, to ring his Order's knell,
   The passing of the Age of Bronze,
   And of his poesy as well.
Against high hearts no king's writ runs :
   Six Acts avail'd not, twice six Bills   170
   Had not been gag upon such tongues ;
But there's a hoarser note that fills
   The ear held flatways to the ground.
   At first, like thunder in the hills,
Grumbling, it breaks in crashing sound :   175
   That is the cry of slaves broke loose,
   Carrying the fire the country round.
Dragoon'd, despis'd, and by the use
   Of Speenhamlond workt like a beast ;
   Yok'd to a cart, if so they choose   180
Who own him, farmer, squire and priest,
   Bonded to flay him to the bones
   That tithe and rent may be increast—
Who stands or stays to hear his groans ?—
   Who knows or cares what the dog means, 185
   Why now he comes with volley of stones
To break our new-contriv'd machines ?
   They thresh the grain he may not eat,

And thresh it closer than he gleans
The stubble-field ; he sees in it   190
   A way to dock him of his due,
   The last he has—to thresh the wheat
And get a wages for it too.
   He reasons, fed on pulse and bran ;
   He darkly gauges all things new   195
As pattern'd on the devil's plan ;
   Sees squire, priest, farmer, overseer,
   Banded against the working-man—
And has good reason for his fear.
   After machines, the ricks they dare ;   200
   And now by night mad mobsmen cheer
And burn, and in the throbbing glare
   Are wild white faces, hateful glee
   To daunt the Reverend Mr. Hare
And sleek idealists such as he,   205
   Who deem a man but so much grist
   For heavenly milling, apt to be
By Bible-class shap'd optimist.
   To lords in London, no such matter :
   Their remedy is the heavy fist.   210
Out with our bold dragoons to scatter
   The lawless herd !   Up, Mr. Attorney !
   Up, Lords Commissioners, to patter
The Riot Act !   The Law shall learn ye
   To intimidate.   The King's complainant,   215
   The Iron Duke upon his journey.

Down goes his Grace, that staunch Lieutenant,
  New-endow'd Lord of Strathfieldsaye,
And hoists the black flag for his pennant
On Winton jail—a grateful day !   220
  What men he has alive from Spain
  Are swung out of the hero's way;
And lads are hounded o'er the main,
  Herded and huddling in the hulks ;
  There are but women left to plain,   225
Or some gaunt fugitive that skulks
  The dewy hollows of the Downs.
  So Hodge is cow'd.   They say he sulks,
And lay it to the guile of clowns.
  So much for Hodge's dying stroke,   230
  The uptake now is with the towns.

*ristol
nd
otting-
am,
831.*
Nottingham's castle ends in smoke
  Before the hussars can make bad worse ;
And next the men of Bristol spoke
In fire, whom swords could not disperse   235
  By order'd butchery in a cause
  No longer worth a tinker's curse.
Anarchy makes the Duke to pause
  Who sees our Three Estates so just,
  So past the bettering of laws ;   240
But now he yields because he must,
  And fighting out his worst of fights,
  Shakes from his shoes his country's dust.

THE SONG OF THE PLOW

Reform,
1832.

Broke is the fence of kingly rights
    Which Edward, little lov'd in Wales,   245
    Set long ago, that the shire's knights
Might dock his barons of their vails :
    Gone where such gear must go whose users
    Make their game, " Heads I win—or tails."
Gross Henry made his heirs the losers   250
    When he, to render smooth his way,
    Packt his Parliaments : his new Sirs
Would send to pack their king one day.
    Henry left traitor Charles discover
    Packing a game that two could play.   255
From the foul spawn of that self-lover
    There gadded like a fungus growth
    That web of franchise England over
Which drain'd our land of blood and blowth
    The King first packt his Parliament,   260
    And that the electorate ; but both
Together workt to one end—Rent !
    They shackled Hodge and suckt him dry
    For that ; for that to war they went,
For war will keep the prices high.   265
    For that they voted ; and for that
    A man had seats to sell, or buy,
And claim'd a Seat as where you sat,
    Not where a people needed it.
    There might be cover for a rat :   270
It served—so it was served by writ.

182

My lord went down, or sent his valet,
And Bagge M.P. went up to sit :
You bought these things by auction-mallet ;
   They went, like livings, with the land—   275
   Corruption, Simony, what d'ye call it ?
They are so old, they sure must stand !
   But now the very stones cry, Tear 'em,
   Send 'em the way that Bristol plann'd.
Down like a house of cards goes Barum,   280
   Down goes the Cornish voting wedge ;
   Gatton and Grampound, Bedwyn, Sarum,
Down with them all ! Stub up the hedge
   That holds a nation tied and prone
   Under the heel of Privilege !   285
But let not Hodge look for his own
   Ere fifty years of talk be o'er ;
   The men who take the emptied throne
Love him than they of old no more,
   Sweat him no less. Hodge and his plows 290
   Are *corpus vile* for their lore.
What ! Mountain-travail and this mouse ?
   The hunger-gallèd centuries
   Split Upper House from Lower House
And fetch up after all but this,   295
   That Spry the grocer has his whack,
   And cotton-spinning Twill has his ?
'Tis so : the whip for Hodge's back
   Is now of logic 'stead of twigs ;

Small help to him that both can crack,⁣   300
And comfort small that lordly Whigs
  Sit cheek by jowl in rueful case
  With Radicals set up in gigs.
Manchester has a barren face
  For Hodge who plows the lonely acres ;   305
  Laissez-faire keeps him in his place
Or drives him join the peace's breakers :
  Then trust the Law know how to deal
  Without induction from the Quakers.
But here's a something he will feel   310
  When dealt to him by *à priori*,
  A turn of wheat bread for his meal
After long battling for the theory
  That Rent is not best serv'd by him
  Who starves a hind to fatten a Tory.   315
But such a grace still glimmers dim
  While rise the Union's iron walls,
  On Speenhamland a comment grim.

BOOK XII

THE SEETHING

BOOK XII : THE SEETHING

O QUIET land I love so well,
   And see so lovely as I roam
   By woody holt or grassy swell,
Or where the sun strikes new-turn'd loam
   To gleaming bronze, or by the shore   5
   Follow the yellow'd curves of foam,
And see the wrinkl'd sand grow frore
   As gives the tide.   O free and brave,
   Send me to sing the fate in store
For thine and mine as thou wouldst have,   10
   Earn'd by my brothers' rough-hewn way,
   And by my brothers in the grave !
My fate I thank who let me stay
   Just so long in my stricken land
   To see my English rise up gay   15
And with our Normans take their stand,
   Equal in peril, so resolv'd
   To break the menace of the brand.
Strange, by that stroke the knots be solv'd
   Which held two nations rop'd apart   20
   While eight slow centuries revolv'd

187

THE SONG OF THE PLOW

And kinship ossified at heart !
  Yet so it was, from German lust
  That English flower of grace could start.

Victoria,
1837.

When she whose star thro' all the dust   25
  Of years to be will shine forth clear,
  Naming Victoria the Just,
Took up her yoke of sixty year,
  Poor Hodge, on sufferance in his garth,
  'Twixt work and Workhouse apt to steer,   30
Stay'd in his gleaning of good earth,
  Stay'd in the reek of tedded hay,
  To heed the bells and share their mirth.

1838,
28 June.

They crown'd a queen on that June day ;
  The heat lay heavy on the weald ;
  But he must on, and might not stay   35
While the slow wains were in the field
  Half-piled, and horses fly-madden'd
  Shook in the shafts, or trod and squeal'd.
Send her victorious, give good end   40
  To all her battles, may she find
  The God of Jacob for her friend !
So might he sing with steadfast mind,
  And deem the prayer as good as any,
  Reckoning kings and all that kind   45
As bald-faced heads upon a penny,
  Changing in feature, not in skill
  To make one do the work of many.

THE SEETHING

Her ministries might form and fill—
    Melbourne or Peel or Palmerston—   50
    Appointed as electors will
On hustings, which he gapes upon,
    And marks beer flow and banners dip,
    And sees Squire Western or Lord John
Exchange with farmer grip for grip;   55
    Or hears their breathless periods
    Hailing a newfound partnership
'Twixt men of birth and men of clods,
    Wherefrom it seems, there must arise
    New Heaven, new Earth, new men, new gods. 60
It may be so : Hodge rubs his eyes
    And picks his work up where he dropt it ;
    Serene the field of fallow lies
After the shaven sheep have cropt it :
    Work is eternal, so is want ;   65
    No 'lection yet has ever stopt it,
Though sure is each new postulant
    That he has found for every hole
    The very peg you ought to plant.

Hodge
and the   How stood our man what time the Poll   70
Poor   Went humming, full of days to be ?
Law.   He had the House instead of the Dole,
Nine shillings a week for all his fee ;
    One or two more in harvest-time,
    His hovel his while he could see   75

THE SONG OF THE PLOW

His way to work ; but past his prime,
   Darkly before him loom'd the day
   When eld is treated as a crime.
Yet in the village the young ones play ;
   Yet courting swain woos bashful maid ;   80
   Yet children come the ancient way,
And man and wife are not afraid,
   Nor know themselves as rarely nobbled
   As ever when the Norman's blade
Ruled England, and a man was hobbled   85
   To Manor. Worse his present store,
   For when his chin is silver-stubbled
They shift him from his cottage-door
   And send him pack. The house is tied,
   But he—he's old, his day is o'er ;   90
The Union takes him : let him bide.

The Rail,   O changeless fate and changeless dream
1839.   Within a changing countryside !
Now is the hour of rail and steam,
   And still our conscripts of the soil   95
   Work on the glebe thro' shower and gleam
To furnish others' corn and oil
   For pence a day, without a thought
   That that was theirs whereon they toil,
And without them the land is nought ;   100
   Nor guessing how the iron road
   Might cost them more than ever it brought.
It brought the city and its god

190

THE SEETHING

Into the realm of grass and sky.
The horse at noon which stands anod   105
Or flings his bag of chaff on high
  Pricks up his ears to hear the rattle
  Or see the vivid steam fling by ;
And the day comes when Hodge must battle
  With work alone, and leave his son   110
  Prove whether men must plod like cattle
And lie cast out, by work foredone,
  Unown'd, unneeded, one with sorrow,
  No spit of land to call their own.

The Call of Town. The town calls men from garth and furrow ; 115
  The land is emptied of its youth :
  The dear-won sweets of earth to borrow,
The use of love, the meed of truth,
  Work's sake, the holiness of rest,
  The soil which owns men sib and couth— 120
Stifled by maggots in a nest !
  There where the labour of men's hands
  It render'd grimly, without zest,
And Rage holds Grief in iron bands,
  And Grief on fetters wrings her teeth ; 125
  Where women look on broken strands
Of faith and promise bruis'd beneath
  The devil's hoof of circumstance ;
  And the pale children scold and seethe,
Too early thrown a crumb to chance—   130
  There let Hodge send his son to school,

To win by hate what sufferance wants!
There mote he learn how tyrants rule,
   How men, like masters, make array,
   While Honour has her bosomful   135
Of shame, and Sloth need not dismay :
   The game goes to the longer purse
   Or stouter stomach this new way.
There mote he learn how ill spells worse,
   How masters' bad blood makes men's high, 140
   How money-grudging ministers,
And Strike is Lock-out's mimicry :
   The war of waiting, the war of food,
   To fight with famine, and let no cry,
As if a man in his own blood   145
   Should drown his foe, or for oriflamme
   Tear out his heart and find that good
To rally his friends with ere death came.
   There mote he learn the lust of rage,
   Or from his shoulders shrug the blame, 150
Saying, God has us in a cage,
   Here is no scope for armistice ;
   The womb's remorseless tutelage,
Moulding what shall be by what is,
   Gives meat to tooth that has no pity,   155
   The manna of unrighteousness.
Young lad, young lass, the fresh or pretty,
   What shall they have who drove despair
   To the bitter schooling of the city ?

THE SEETHING

anches-
r Logic. Manchester still says, *Laissez-faire* ;   160
    Manchester, strong in Parliament,
    Says, Trade has made us what we are ;
Money breeds quicklier than rent.
    Let land go sick and men grow sallow
    In humming mill, in gallery bent   165
To win the coal where seams run shallow :
    Here is the future, England ! Trade,
    And leave the farmer's acres fallow.
All things conspire, the rails are laid,
    Great ships will bear you off by steam ;   170
    The mill-hand flickers like a blade
When work is done ; the mill-girls deem
    The country wench a wanting-wit
    Who never saw the gas-lamps gleam,
Nor suckt an orange in the pit,   175
    Nor in the music-hall gave tongue
    When Champagne Charlie ruffled it.
The town is open to the young ;
    As for the land, 'tis very old ;
    Let Granfer go on scattering dung,   180
Working for ha'pence in the cold ;
    Fortune lies laughing in the town,
    Whose streets, they say, are paved with gold.
So old Hodge dreams upon his down,
    And young Hodge trips the primrose way, 185
    And hunts the iris-bubble blown
Ever before him, till he's gray ;

And shredding like the morning mist
The gaudy thing is whiskt away
To lure another optimist.   190
  Fast on his glebe old Hodge is rooted,
  Too stiff to ope his horny fist
To catch at what from town is bruited,
  Or else too slow ; and after him
  Still comes another, his way suited   195
Serving the land, his thought too dim
  To appraise his lot. He judges better
  That he to Nature it should trim,
What though the galling of his fetter
  Should seal a callous on the mind,   200
  And numb the soul to save a tetter.
He could not learn how wrongs may bind
  Man unto man ; how you may rob
  Your own kin to advance your kind,
And so do well. He swell'd a mob,   205
  But never serried in phalanx,
  Nor rais'd a Union from his club —
God bless him and his sturdy flanks !

Free Trade, 1845–6.   But if God see a pack well speeded
  And let a singling hound draw blanks ?   210
None the less Hodge plugg'd on unheeded
  By Gods above and Whigs below ;
  Yet won the corn he sorely needed
When Cobden struck for Trade his blow,

THE SEETHING

And Peel struck, and by *gran' rifiuto*—   215
Broke troth, but sav'd his honour so.
Bentinck might rage and Dizzy blow to
    A flame his bile white-hot and scathing—
    Withal the world knows, as he knew too,
That should he catch the Whigs a-bathing   220
    He'd steal their clothes, as steal he did :
    Such grigs hold politics a plaything.
Natheless the Sliding-scale hath slid
    To nothingness ; there's wheat galore.
    Hodge gets his gallon of white bread   225
Where he'd had rye and bran before,
    And sometimes horsebeans for his pain,
    And sometimes none—God pity the poor !
Yet there were men, and are again,
    Who cried the commonwealth betray'd,   230
    Saying, " Keep prices up amain
If you would see high wages paid :
    Why, what if bread goes up a penny ?
    Think of your wages, and our trade."
But Hodge : " My father hadn't any   235
    When corn was up in Thirty-one.
    They mout have hanged un, one of many,
But he slipt out.   What had he done
    But sought to feed hisself and mother
    Who had no milk to feed me on ?   240
An' now you raise a moil and pother
    To bring me back those hungry days :

Tell me the farmer is my brother !
Ask him a Saturday what he says,
    Seeing as the hay sold smartish well,   245
    Whether my money he mid raise.
Raise me my ——, and bid to hell
    The likes of me : 'tis what he'd do—
    And me stone-breaking for a spell ! "
Hodge has a rhetoric, like his brew,   250
    A something bitter, with a smack
    Of camomile about it too.
Redoubtable ! whose quips would crack
    While the rheumatics ache and twitch
    About his own down-driven back.   255

1851.   Yet trade goes briskly : we grow rich
    Tho' land lie lean and peasants dwindle ;
    Within another hemistich
You'll hear enough your thoughts to kindle.
    They raise the Glasshouse on the green   260
    To hymn the triumph of the spindle
Over the plow. Alas ! good Queen,
    You hail'd a flashlight for a star :
    " The greatest glory Peace has seen,"
Quod you ! Come three years we had war ; 265
    And on war's back a Mutiny
    There where our servants Hindus are,
Strange folk, who strive for liberty
    By methods we have consecrate,

To make men slaves lest slaves we be.   270
Thus our old masters serv'd their state,
    And thus our burgesses have learn'd
ess of   The trick of it.   You dar'd your fate
ire. In some far land; your fortunes turn'd :
    Red-sworded then you claim'd the span   275
    Your heavy-mailèd fist had earn'd.
How else was Hodge made William's man,
    Save by the rascal's *hardiesse?*
    How else came we by Hindostan ?
How else do weasels, to possess   280
    The rabbit's blood ?   A little lower
    Than angels, we !   A generous guess.
Tarnish is on us, how we scour
    And rinse—yet God be thankt, with mirth
    Our men serve Freedom at this hour !   285
dom. Regent of men, of Mother Earth
    The spouse, to whom she and her brood
    Stand to do service, nothing worth
Save as free gift, for reason good !
    Say, hath not Hodge beseem'd thee well,   290
    Sounding thy name across the flood,
When, bond by free, he fought and fell,
    Fought on, and lived, and did endure
    Against the despot's manacle ?
See how his birthright does inure,   295
    That even unfree he dare not brook
    A hand against his Cynosure,

197

A troth-plight broke, a saucy look !
  What makes *he* now of Englishmen
  Who our tough mettle so mistook ?   300
Nought of this horror lay in ken
  What time Law's slow-enlarging tide
  Swam to the mark where now my pen
May fathom what it dim-descried
  Centuries past, when Bonaccord   305
  Padded about the countryside—

Ballot and Franchise, 1872–1883. This namely, Hodge and Hodge's lord
  Stand level by the Ballot-box.
  Level ? So once, by cruse unpour'd,
Stood long-bill'd stork and short-nebb'd fox ; 310
  And stork fed full, the while his guest
  Tipt not the vessel on the rocks.
What more than franchise have the best,
  Say you, who have not read my scrolls :
  What need he but his voice attest ?   315
Vote-catching's in, that game of polls—
  Here's a new voter worth attention.
  From Whig and Tory dangle doles,
Allotments here, an old-age pension ;
  Insurance, or that blessed thing,   320
  Tariff, as poverty-prevention.
The Ring. Even as you'll see an auction-ring
  Bid high, bid low, nor guess a knock-out,
  So at the poll with shop-dressing :
The rival traders set their stock out,   325

Having agreed to pool the plunder.
How comes it else one Court will lock out
Those whom it stands to serve? A wonder!
To grant land-holding by an Act,
And split the awarding of it asunder—   330
'Twixt whom? 'Twixt who had and who lackt?
Nay, but 'twixt squire at home and squire
In County Council! Sober fact.
So this: the village-mote's desire
May not by village be effected;   335
No, but by them who own or hire
The villagers—'tis true, elected—
True, but who knows his country's quips
Will know why Hodge is not neglected
At 'lection times, by ladyships.   340

*dge at
ction.*

Then nostrums fly for Hodge's fancy:
A tax on corn now! Best of tips.
By some sleight-handed nigromancy
Wages will run upstairs to meet it.
Some say the thing is more than chancy;   345
You need but name it to defeat it.
These offer land; those say, " Absurd!
What's land to Hodge? He cannot eat it."
But none so far as I have heard
Say, " He is wrong'd; let wrong be righted."   350
Ransom indeed's an ugly word
For lips of councillors beknighted,
Or set upon the broad high-road

199

THE SONG OF THE PLOW

Where limber tongue may be requited.
And Hodge, who never feared the goad,   355
   Has for all this fine talk his qualms :
   Long has he journey'd with his load
And no man yet has found him balms
   To ease him gall'd or lead him blind,
   Or cross with silver his hard palms.   360
He doubts, and cunning comes to mind ;
   Then baffled touts who lookt to buy
   His interest for their usury find
He is not handy to the ply.
   They wring the pipe, he will not dance ;   365
   They toss their hands : the rogue is sly !
On one and all you look askance,
   And it's no wonder ; yet it's true,
   Had you the hang o't, now's your chance
To win your own back—if you knew !   370
   But you are as you always were
   Since on the chalk-hills throve the yew,
On your own feet, tho' they go bare,
   Wise in the lore of wind and weather,
   Patient and mild, with pride to spare,   375
Pliant as withe—and tough as leather !

The Carrion-Cryers.
   Now, as when wool again shows thick
   On back of ewe and teg and wether
A goodly colony of tick
   Will feed and fasten, so now swarm   380

200

THE SEETHING

They who a sustenance can pick
Out of man's hankering for harm.
  Hodge is a voter, and can read,
  Thanks to the length of Forster's arm—
Out then, ye Dungflies, buzz and breed ;   385
  Cozen 'em, tempt 'em, bleed 'em, flay 'em !
  We are the mongers that they need,
Offal and carrion to purvey 'em.
  Base is the slave whom doubts deter :
  Men whisper rumours—why not bray 'em? 390
" Pictures in Court—The Ha'p'ny Blur ! "
  Is Hodge a right koprophagite ?
  Behold his right koprographer.
O my young men, when times are tight
  Do for your halfpence all a penny may.   395
  Be false, be true, but oh, be bright ;
If short of slaver, yet be venomy :
  Hint shame broadcast if none appears !
  How shall Hodge cope with this new enemy ?

Century's The land is sick and full of fears.   400
End.   And you, O hopeless, heartsick ye,
  Sick with your surfeit of salt tears
And heritage of agony.
  What have we made of you, O Earth,
  Since of your lap you made us free ?   405
For our blithe lads and girls of worth
  Their home a place of pilgrimage,

Where sorrow's finger points their mirth
The haven of their failing age.
  Hungry, they shall have stones for meat ; 410
  Homeless, the bald-eyed Poorhouse cage—

Discrep-
ancy. What time his lordship in his seat
  Born of a woman, even as they,
  Has three tall men to help him eat :
One to take his platter away, 415
  One to put a clean one down,
  And one the couple to survey.
What has he to share with a clown,
  Should one seek his doors of pride,
  Having brav'd the gateward's frown, 420
To hob and nob, sit side by side !
  As well expect the Penitent Thief
  See gerent of the Crucified
In Canterbury's mitred chief
  As Hodge, whose thatch is tumbling in, 425
  Go to his lordship for relief.
Here is the mischief—whose the sin ?
  Who will bring Hodge and lord acquaint ?
  And can the leopard change his skin ?

Sirs, since your fathers earn'd the taint, 430
  Seeing that they ground the face of the poor,
  And now are gone, sinner and saint,
Therefore this woe is at your door ;
  Therefore on you the heavy stour

THE SEETHING

That he who has shall have no more.   435
Inheritance was your strong tower,
    And there's inheritance of wrong
    As well as right ; this is the hour
When you must take it up, for strong
    The weak is made ; and to his hand   440
    The whirligigs of time belong.
Face you the Angel with the brand,
    His eyes unbound, his longsword naked ;
    Hear him : Your fathers held this land,
A trust upon it, but they brake it.   445
    Now it is escheat, now the sand
    Is run. 'Tis Hodge's. Let him take it.

ENVOY

NEW DOMESDAY

ENVOY: NEW DOMESDAY

The Fond
Dream.

THERE was a time—how fondly dream'd
    And long ago ! whenas I thought
    To see your sufferance redeem'd
By the same use whereby 'twas wrought ;
    And in the mind I still'd the heart   5
    To endure the woe for what it brought.
But who shall woe from woe dispart,
    Or how ill blood with ill agree ?
    Or shall a new wound salve the smart
Of an old wound ?   Alas, to see   10
    You sweep remorseless as a tide
    Over the land from sea to sea,
Men by long grievance justified
    To put down tyranny—and in the act
    Whelming the proud, to ape their pride !   15

The
Awaken-
ing.

Keener revenge and nobler pact
    Were yours, to hold your antient wrong
    Nothing beside the staring fact.
You faced the dawn, I knew you strong—
    Even in that hour the German Death,   20
    Like the bright sword by one hair swung,
Was pulsing time out with short breath ;

THE SONG OF THE PLOW

And every man must stand to vow
How he would live, and in what faith.

Hodge
chooses.
See there upon the hill's broad brow,   25
   Where first you saw him, Hodge at gaze ;
   A bondsman once, a hireling now,
Half conscious of the broadening ways :
   Look well on him, how he comes down
   To front the terror of these days.   30
Over the sea the fame is blown,
   A shadow'd fear not yet a shape,
   Which husht the tumult of the town
And made men stand like fools agape :
   A doubt, a dread, a Can it be ?   35
   A wild look all ways for escape ;
But like a storm scourging the sea,
   A blur of fog which was not cloud,
   With spindrift edges flying free
Like smoke, and underneath that shroud   40
   Riotous waters, livid, wan,
   Swirling and hissing, wave acrowd
On waves' back—onward the news ran
   On a chill wind, and men abasht
   Lookt at each other, man on man,   45
And waited till the first drop splasht,
   While the great wave of horror grew,
   Tower'd over Europe, cream'd and crasht
Over his England ; and Hodge knew

NEW DOMESDAY

The time was come when he must choose   50
For God, or no-God, even he too ;
For now it was not to refuse.
   Little reckt he of such high work
   As made the Presses hum with news
Of England bottling like a cork   55
   The Baltic peoples ; vain to speak
   To him of Balkan or the Turk :
He knows them less than he knows Greek.
   Out of his simple mouth 'tis spoken,
   " The mighty have opprest the weak ;   60
The word was past and has been broken ;
   Belgium was free and now is not—
   Up ! Are we free ? Then by that token
Free we the slaves by powder and shot ! "
   He made no boast, grudged no old scar,   65
   Sought nothing that he had not got,
But took his place affronting war,
   The slow, the patient child of Earth,
   By them on whom a happier star
Shone to forecast a happier birth :   70
   All brothers now ! for thus, one race,
   We met the odds with decent mirth.
See them swing out, of open face,
   Clear-eyed and careless, having made
   The Great Assent ; with quickening pace,   75
With laughter and song ! Ah, woodland glade,
   How are you silent in your gold !

914,
Autumn
nd
Winter.

209   P

THE SONG OF THE PLOW

Ah, sunburnt hill and orchard-shade,
Ah, river twinkling manifold
    Thro' meadow flats and meadowsweet,   80
    These lads are young and ye are old,
Withal ye gave them of your teat ;
    For they are England even as ye,
    Bone of your bone, meat of your meat—
Weep not, but hold a solemn glee   85
    In that clear courage and deep pride
    Which call'd your sons of each degree
To dare the terror side by side,
    Norman and English, sinking name
    In one—and that Tyrannicide.   90
See there the poacher of the game,
    And there the master of men and pheasants,
    And there the man who makes them tame
And drives them over guns for presents—
    Who shall care now such blood to class   95
    And docket men as lords or peasants ?

Tantæne Travail'd the Chaos to this pass ?
Iræ?   To this end was the orb conceiv'd ?
    To this end from the stirring mass
The Alpine backbone was upheav'd ?   100
    Was it for this end took their shape
    The well-lov'd fields, the many-sheav'd,
Or man, the master, raised his nape—
    To raven all down one red chasm,

And sink his kind, who had slough'd the ape, 105
To new abysmal protoplasm ?
   There was no horror like to this,
   The wide world in one lockt orgasm—
Not when on cliff-girt Salamis
   By every sea-road Persian hordes   110
   Converging, focuss'd upon Greece ;
Nor when the storm of Saracen swords
   Swept a broad road thro' swathes of men
   And rais'd new nations and new lords
From Egypt to the bar of Spain ;   115
   Nor when the glutted vulture preen'd
   His neck, and saw the Polish fen
Blacken'd and silent, and well-glean'd !
   Those men with men in battle spoke,
   And men like men in death were keen'd ; 120
But now they are blown away like smoke,
   Legions of men by mine upsprung,
   Or in foul fog are merged, to choke
And foam away their sodden lung :
   Now man is minister of Death   125
   Like him who over Egypt flung
His flaggy wing, as Scripture saith,
   And slew the firstborn.   Even so,
   Not peace, but a sword, said Nazareth ;
But we : " He spake it long ago   130
   And we have prov'd the saying vain."
   Now stands He justified : we know

THE SONG OF THE PLOW

The beast in man is not yet slain.
　　Weep not your dead, they are eloquent ;
　　They grave their *Credo* deep in pain ;　　135
High faith in high deed will find vent ;
　　With each bright drop of golden blood
　　We blazon our New Testament.

An Old
Thought.
As up by Kennetside I rode
　　From Newbury to Savernake,　　140
　　I thought what sounds had charged her flood
Since Norman William's sword fell slack—
　　What cheers of triumph and what groans
　　This funded earth had echoed back,
This soil made deep with English bones,　　145
　　Made rich with blood of Englishmen,
　　Whose rede lies graven in the stones
A-litter on the hillside !　Then,
　　Grieving the willow-border'd mead,
　　Grieving the flower-haunted fen,　　150
The broad-eav'd farms, the nobly-treed,
　　The eddying river stemm'd with mills,
　　My eyes sought comfort in their need
And found the everlasting hills,
　　And rested there.　" Let purple ink　　155
　　Content," said I, " the eagle-quills ;
A drabber fluid shall mine drink
　　To hymn the plowshare, not the brand ;
　　I'll voice the tears upon the brink

That often dript upon the hand.   160
  And if it be that all the sighs
  I hear behind the brazen band
Shall be assuaged ; and if men's eyes
  Look forthright cheerly once again,
  With prescience may my pen be wise,   165
And my heart apt to tongue the strain
  Of England held by English folk,
  And English folk not cleft in twain !
What's Empire but a sable smoke
  Crowning a smother of ill-content ?   170
  Lazarus sore in a silk cloak,
With sharp bones staring thro' a rent !
  Who, knowing the leper's maddening itch
  Beneath the stiff habiliment,
Would not give all that made him rich   175
  For one clear day that saw him sane,
  Whole man, altho' without a stitch
To cover him from wind and rain ? "
  Then, where the forest on the ridge
  Thrusts his green shoulder to the plain,   180
I saw the end of Privilege.

A New Dream.

A blood-red rainbow over-archt
  Our cloven land, which like a bridge
Our men cross'd over.—Faint and parcht,
  Blind, maim'd, tormented, spent and dim,   185
  The halting broken legions marcht,

Helping each other, with what limb
  Remain'd to one, by other lost.
  So lean'd the legless man to him
Who yet had his, for propping-post,   190
  And the blind turn'd his empty face
  To him who saw ; and so they crost
The gulf upon that Bridge of Grace
  Together, brothers in accord,
  With thousands more in the same case.   195
O crowning light upon the sword !
  Here, of these men of English earth,
  Which is the servant, which the lord,
And whose the fee-simple by birth ?
  Upon the bridge stood One who said :   200
  " All Englishmen are now one worth,
And all one kindred with the dead,
  And share the goodly heritage
  For which their forefathers have bled.
Presume not palter with the gage   205
  They lifted, nor your own forget :
  You stinted not the noble rage
They had ; now, with the sword still wet,
  See England conquer'd by her own,
  And carve the conquest out, and set   210
The cantle due of vill and town."

New Domes-day.

Then I saw Sarum, in my dream,
  Breasting her open sea of down,

214

Whose ripples are the shadow and gleam
   As the clouds hang, or drive and pass ;   215
   And there the hero-host did seem
A countless flock upon the grass.
   High on the rampart thron'd a king,
   Prouder than ever William was,
Whose cope was like an eagle's wing   220
   Folded, adone with lean and soar,
   Whose sceptre-hand had no great ring,
Whose orb was crystal clear and hoar :
   I saw the crown upon his head
   Flame, though no diamond it bore—   225
" This is no earthly king," I said.
   Beardless he was, and calm, and grave ;
   His face was like a God's ; he had
The ease that Caryatids have,
   Who drink deep bosomfuls of air,   230
   Holding a temple architrave.
His speaking voice was still and rare,
   Like a wind's calling thro' far trees
   High on an upland stark and bare,
More constant than the fretful sea's ;   235
   And thus he spake from the green hill
   To all those waiting companies :—
" That which made England makes her still :
   You who have ransom'd by shed blood
   Your right to harvest what you till,   240
Your right to hold what you make good,

Let right be done henceforth to all,
That all may be a brotherhood."
Then thron'd he there imperial,
  And one by one the conquerors came,   245
  As he was cried by herald tall,
And told his title and his claim ;
  And when his deed stood manifest
  A trumpet shrilled it like a flame.
Then said the King : "Tell now the best   250
  England can do for your deserving ;"
  And ere he named it all the rest
Stood with wet eyes their mate observing,
  Waiting to clinch the guesswork shrewd
  They'd made of him with faith unswerving.   255

So before all a young man stood
  With flickering lids and chin tiltwise,
  As of one listening in a wood
To feel which way the sunlight lies.
  "I look no more upon the sun,"   260
  Said he. "I gave my pair of eyes.
Give me a cottage, a handy one
  Where I can hear the youngsters pass,
  And have a portion in the fun."
Another said : "Give me all grass ;   265
  For since the German-hounded Turk
  Bit me a leg, the man I was
Is not the man I bring to work.
  But with some grassland I'll make shift

216

To live by raising stot or stirk,   270
Or sheep may be, if I have thrift."
   Next a young man stood, very fair,
   Calm-eyed, who had the Norman lift
To his proud head, and lookt the heir
   To centuries of rule. Said he,   275
   " I took what came, and had no care
For how or wherefore. Now I see
   What I can do. I want no lands—
   Give me some work—make use of me.
I have my eyes and pair of hands ;   280
   There should be ventures left for such
   As look for them, while England stands."
He blusht for talking overmuch,
   Then took his task and gave his room
   To one who hung upon his crutch,   285
A sharp-faced twitcher like a groom,
   Who, broken in the Dardanelles,
   Made thus his homely bid for doom :
" Sir, this is all their blessèd shells
   Have left me, but I'm not dead yet.   290
   If I could have the *Ring of Bells*
I'd still make out my keep to get—
   And maybe pay my funeral."
   Then came a woman pale with fret,
In widow-weeds, a woman small :   295
   " I sent my man and my four sons
   After the drum. I sent them all.

They fell before the German guns.
    What can you give to bring them back ? ''
    Bitter reproach was in her tones ;   300
But the King comforted her lack,
    Saying, " Blessèd are you who spend !
    A festal robe is this your black,
Witness that more than life you lend
    Unto the land that gave you birth.   305
    Greater love is there not, nor end
More pious ; nor can mannish worth
    Climb to the height whereon you stand.
    Live you, love on, and sweeten earth."
Her eyes swam full at that command,   –   310
    And deep she breathed ; and there was no man
    But did her honour in our land.
And next came one, led by a woman,
    Young, with the face of a hurt child,
    His shockt eyes wavering and not human; 315
And oft he flincht, and next he smil'd
    As if he had caught himself.   Then pity
    Set him to weep himself beguil'd.
Anon his nurse :   " Arras the city
    Was rain'd upon by shot and shell ;   320
    Thereby this lad once brave and witty
Became the thing you see him still.
    Ten nights and days he might not sleep,
    But serv'd the apprenticeship of Hell—
Then a long scream, the earth did leap,   325
    Men were toss'd out like scatter'd dung,

And lay as wreckage ; but one did creep
On all-fours where this lad was flung,
   Thinking he liv'd, and dragg'd him out,
   Pitying his mother—and he so young.   330
Now he is witless, at a shout
   Will start and fumble for his gun ;
   Or he will cry and rock about
For no plain reason."   That thron'd One
   Set hand on him, and by the chin   335
   Lifted his face ; and " Oh, my son,"
Said he, " why, what a work, to win
   The sun again to gladden you,
   And of your tears draw mist to spin
A veil half golden and half blue   340
   Across the past, until it seem
   Like to the radiant deed it drew,
Such a high deed as young men dream
   But not achieve.   But you, my lad,
   Are happier yet, than yet you deem."   345
Then to his nurse, " Go on," he said,
   " Turn to your work ; but ours shall be
   Pattern'd on yours, as good and glad."
And all the host held like the sea
   On burning noons of southern calm   350
   When the light flecks innumerably
The little freshets, and like balm
   A steady wind blows from the West,
   And softly wave the fronds of palm,
And the stork sleeps, bill sunk in breast.   355

THE SONG OF THE PLOW

*The
Marvel.*

Now when of all that mighty host
There was no claim left unexprest,
The King stood motionless and lost
    In memories thronging ; and I strove
    Myself with wonder, which was most   360
To wonder, that so mighty love
    These men had testified (with those
    Who, dying, testified above),
Or this appraisal of their throes
    As they themselves had figured it.   365
    " Now let them learn how England goes
To war," methought, "and how is quit !
    Blood, nerve and limb her men will give,
    And keep alone that which makes sweet
Blood, nerve and limb, the zest to live   370
    And love and labour on the ground,
    Holding their old prerogative
To stand alone, to no man bound ;
    Then, with that unexhausted fire,
    Homeward to where their fathers found   375
No man held worthy of his hire
    They come—and all they ask shall be
    A lugg of ground, a bite, a byre
To hold a heifer.   O ye free,
    It was for this your fathers plow'd   380
    The flinty fields of misery,
That you should in their pride be proud
    And for their wretchedness ask no fee,
    But vow yourselves because they vow'd,

220

And hold the faith they died to see   385
  Trac'd on the snow-white field in blood,
  The burning cross of Liberty ! "
Now, as I thought, the great King stood,
  And over all the peopled plain
  There fell that hush, as when a wood   390
Is sober'd suddenly, and the rain
  Drives over it, and we stand still
  And see the tree-tops all astrain,
And hear the wind, but no wind feel.
  And then he spoke, and his far voice   395
  Was like that same wind over a hill :

The
Award.   " You, for whose deeds no organ noise
  Will throb *Te Deum*, yet in whom
  The great Arbitrament lay in choice,
And as you chose should fall the Doom—   400
  Now hear ; the land you have redeem'd
  Is yours by conquest, to resume.
Not for your profit have you schemed,
  Nor ventur'd all for your reward ;
  None, since the Corsican, has dream'd   405
To pass your seas, and none has dar'd
  Since Philip's galleons hemm'd the West
  And Drake steered out from Plymouth Hard,
And the South-West wind did the rest—
  No, but you knew us inviolate,   410
  Yet stood for them that were opprest ;
Thus you serv'd more than King or State,

THE SONG OF THE PLOW

Since you serv'd all men far or near,
  Discerning Freedom in debate !
Hard won is she ; hard earn'd the fear   415
  Of men gone mad with greed and boast ;
  Blessèd is she, and yet more dear
The men who won her ; and yet most
  Blessèd of all the land new won—
  Yours by the sword from coast to coast.   420
As I decree so be it done :
  A tithe of his land let each man spare,
  Or of his money if he have none ;
In giving be he debonair,
  As if his left serv'd his right hand   425
  And fear'd to be the last to share.
Thus Hodge shall win at last his land—
  You, Earl of forty thousand acres,
  Give your four thousand ; you who stand
Master of five, for the new takers   430
  Give your two roods, to avoid the shame
  That England scorn her Empire-makers ;—
For such they are who fought and came
  Back to their land of birthright old,
  Masters by right of all men's fame."   435
God speed the plow ! The tale is told.

  9 *March* 1916.

NOTES

NOTES

THERE can be no attempt to write a History of England in these notes. The poem has been designed to be self-sufficient from its own standpoint, and to present the passing hours and years as they might have appeared to Hodge himself, misty and full of dim rumours, with occasional flashes of things in the doing. But as it is necessarily concentrated, prevented from for ever striking A before it can strike B, it is bound to be allusive and to take great names for granted. The notes which follow are intended to explain whatever may be difficult to the reader of average instruction, to supplement the text-books, and occasionally to justify what may seem a doubtful or a hard saying. Archaic words or phrases will also be expounded.

PRELUDE, line 50. The lines in italics are part of an old song, of which the whole will be found in *Ancient English Christmas Carols*, collected by Edith Rickert. She dates it as "before 1536," which, to say the least, it undoubtedly is. I myself believe it to be fifteenth century.

Id. l. 88. The *warp* is land formed by the silt of a river : here, the sand or mud which is raked up to dam water-courses and flood the meadows. See Wright, *English Dialect Dictionary*, s.v.

Id. l. 111. A *borstal* is a sunk grass-road leading from the chalk-down to the plain : supposed to be an ancient cattle-way, and possibly neolithic in origin.

Id. l. 123. *Great Christopher*. The image of this holy giant was usually depicted on the north wall of the church, so that it might be the first thing seen on entrance. Saint Christopher was prophylactic against accident. Several frescoes of him remain in country churches.

NOTES

Id. l. 205. *Saint Use.* Use-and-Wont, or Custom, has been the Englishman's fortress against tyranny or aggression from the beginning, and still is. If any man doubt it, let him try to stop up a footpath in his parish.

Id. l. 259. *Theows* = slaves.

BOOK I. line 5. *Never a one / Of English blood . . .* Perhaps there is an exception. Queen Elizabeth was as nearly British as might be. Her father had British blood in him, and her mother, though probably ot Norman or Picard origin, may have had some too.

I. l. 39. *Dives-on-Sea.* At this little town, in the mouth of the Dive river, the Conqueror's fleet was collected, and here it was held up by wind and weather in August 1066 (Freeman, III. 386).

I. l. 46. *The fyrd* was the militia of the shires, service with which was obligatory on all landholders.

I. l. 47. *The hoar apple-tree.* " Then came William Count of Normandy to Pevensey on St. Michael's-mass-eve ; and immediately after they were ready, they constructed a castle at the town of Hastings. This was then made known to King Harold, and he gathered a great army, and came to meet him at the hoar apple-tree " (*Anglo-Saxon Chronicle*, Rolls Series, II. 167).

I. l. 61. *The Dragon.* This was the flag of Wessex, used as a royal standard by Harold at Senlac.

I. l. 135. *Vill* is a synonym for " manor." It is a Norman word, and every other place-name in Normandy to this day ends in it. Some authorities trace it back to the Roman *villa*, which they believe to have been the origin of the feudal manor. Seebohm and Vinogradoff, to name no others, discuss this hypothesis. According to old English law the term *vill* implied and connoted a manor. See that discussed at length in Pollock and Maitland, *History of English Law*, I. 594 *sqq.*

I. l. 136. *Stoke-Farden.* There is a place called Stoke-Farthing in South Wilts. It had been Stoke in English, was Stoke-Verdun after the Conquest ; then Stoke-Farden, phonetically ; thence Stoke-Farthing, wiseacreishly.

NOTES

I. l. 141. *Boro'*. This was the English burh, still extant as *bury*, another connotation of the Latin *manor* and Norman *vill*.

I. l. 154. *Bovate*. I cannot summarize all the learning on the exact equivalent of this and other quantitative terms. Almost certainly the bovate, virgate, ox-gang, plow-land, and all the rest of them, varied from shire to shire. Vinogradoff, Pollock, Maitland, and other jurists discuss them up and down.

I. l. 181. *Boone* or boon-work was work which the lord could require of his tenants. A sort of rent in kind. It varied in intensity with the nature of the holding ; it was never formally abolished. So late as the time of James I. it was due here and there, and may linger even now where unenfranchised copyhold or customary freehold exists.

I. l. 220. *Cromwell's rod and Hitch's hurt*. Cromwell, on the 10th January 1643, wrote to " the Reverend Mr. Hitch, at Ely," thus : " Mr. Hitch, lest the soldiers should in any tumultuary or disorderly way attempt the reformation of the Cathedral Church, I require you to forbear altogether your choir-service, so unedifying and offensive—and this as you shall answer it, if any disorder should arise thereupon " . . . and more to that effect. Carlyle adds, " Mr. Hitch paid no attention, persisted in his choir-service : whereupon enter the Governor of Ely with soldiers . . . With a rabble at his heels, with his hat on, he walks up to the choir ; says audibly, 'I am a man under authority, and am commanded to dismiss this assembly.' . . . Mr. Hitch has paused for a moment, but seeing Oliver draw back, he starts again : ' As it was in the beginning—— ! ' ' Leave off your fooling, and come down, Sir,' said Oliver, in a voice still audible to this editor ; which Mr. Hitch did now instantaneously give ear to. And so with his whole congregation files out, and vanishes from the field of History " (Carlyle, *Letters and Speeches of Oliver Cromwell*, I. 179).

I. l. 226.   *The empty leagues where Sarum's keep,*
        Islanded lonely in the grass,
        Watches the shepherd and the sheep
        Behold him now . . .

That was in August 1086. " The completion of the Record (Domesday Book), and the great meeting at Sarum of all the landowners in the kingdom, so completely synchronize, and the two are so commonly joined together by almost all the historians of the times, that it is difficult not to believe them to have had an immediate relation to each other" (*Domesday for Wiltshire*, by W. H. Jones, p. xiv. See Freeman upon the same matter, IV. 691).

I. l. 302. *In the strips.* The common-field system of tillage divided up the arable land of the manor into long, narrow strips, so many furrows of the plow. Occupancy of these shifted from year to year : a primitive way of securing rotation of crops which lasted until the end of the eighteenth century. Seebohm's *English Village Community* gives the best account of this husbandry.

I. l. 305. *Villein and neif.* The villein was the *villanus*, or bond-tenant of the manor. *Neif* is the vernacular form of *nativa*, itself the feminine of *nativus*, the man *glebae ascriptus*.

BOOK II. line 28. *The five rivers :* Avon, Wylye, Nadder, Bourne, Ebble.

II. l. 54. *Yelm.* Straw laid out in bundles for thatching.

II. l. 66. *Scutage*. "Next he sought to curb the barons. He instituted Scutage, by which the great feudatories granted a money payment instead of bringing with them to the army hordes of sub-tenants who might obey them rather than the king ; this enabled the king to hire mercenaries, who respected him but not the feudatories" (Pollard, *History of England*, p. 46). That is the gist of it; but see it at length in Stubbs, Miss Norgate, and elsewhere. I take this opportunity of acknowledging my indebtedness to Professor Pollard's masterly and comprehensive essay.

II. l. 129. *Ikenai.* Little or nothing is known of this girl except that she was mother of King Henry's son Geoffrey, Archbishop of York. Her name is recorded by Walter Map, *De Nugis*, V. 6. She has no other name in history, which seems to show that she was of the common people. The tale as I give it is, of course, purely imaginary, though the fact that she was the King's mistress may be accepted.

II. l. 150. *A man of his father's mind.* Geoffrey, Archbishop of York.

NOTES

II. 1. 188. *Charter of Liberties.* Magna Carta, as Professor Pollard neatly says, was "invented by Chief Justice Coke." The Professor insists, very properly, " rather upon its reactionary than its reforming elements." It was, in fact, as he says, a charter of "Liberties," and not of liberty. Upon this important point he is terse and direct (*op. cit.* pp. 53 *sqq.*).

Book III. line 70. *Drudge and drodge.* I owe both rime and fact to Miss E. M. Wright's *Rustic Speech and Folklore* (p. 19), a valuable and delightful book. It is proper to say, however, that my distinction can only be inferred from her.

III. 1. 84. *Bitter brew :* beer, to wit. The first Franciscans, coming from Italy, had no stomach for our staple. They put water to it, to make it thinner, and drank it hot (" De Adventu Minorum " in *Monumenta Franciscana*, I. 7).

III. 1. 188. *The great gray church :* Westminster.

III. 1. 194. *Gai saber :* the art of the Trobadors of Provence and thereabouts. The Court of Henry III was crowded with Southern French.

III. 1. 200. *Grosseteste.* "*Humili de patre et matre sum natus,*" he is reported to have said of himself. A good life of him in the Dictionary and several useful accounts in the Prefaces to the *Lanercost Chronicle*, *Monumenta Franciscana*, and his own *Letters*, in the Rolls Series.

III. 1. 221. *His best work within his land.* I believe that I owe the aphorism contained in this and the next line to Professor Pollard, but can't find it, though I have hunted it up and down his works. It is as obvious as it is usually ignored.

Book IV. line 21. *Loteby :* " a private companion or bedfellow," says Halliwell ; " a concubine." The parson's *loteby* in the fourteenth century had better status than is allowed by that definition. She was his unofficial wife, what the Russians call his civil wife. Practice made the breach of vow a technical offence, as it still does in more than one Catholic country.

IV. 1. 26. *Berkeley's keep :* Berkeley Castle, where Edward II. was murdered.

IV. 1. 96. *Chevisance.* Cotgrave has, " An agreement or composition

NOTES

made ; an end or order set down between a creditor and a debtor." It derives from the old French word *chevir*, to compound, to come to an agreement with a person.

IV. l. 98. *To rob a lady's knee :* when he took Lady Salisbury's garter.

IV. l. 99. *A whore :* Alice Perrers.

IV. l. 104. *Canon of Chimay :* Froissart.

IV. l. 120. *Botes.* These were the local needs which tenants, by custom, were allowed to supply to themselves off the land, chiefly off the woodland. There were hedge-bote, plow-bote, fire-bote, cart-bote, etc.

IV. l. 123. *Jehan le Bel :* the Flemish chronicler who preceded Froissart, and upon whom the greater man founded himself. " *Vénerable homme et discret seigneur Monseigneur Jehan le Bel, chanoine de Saint-Lambert de Liège,*" his pupil calls him. His *Vrayes Chroniques* begin in 1326 and end in 1361.

IV. l. 144. *Routiers :* soldiers on hire, who lived chiefly by pillage.

IV. l. 154. *Garterdom :* " The period of the Black Death was precisely the time when Edward completed a plan which he had begun by the erection of his Round Table at Windsor in 1344. In 1348 he instituted a chapel at Windsor, dedicated to St. George. . . . Within a year this foundation also included the famous Order of the Garter. On St. George's Day the King celebrated the new institution by special solemnities " (*Political History of England*, III, 380). The Black Death had begun in 1348.

IV. l. 177. *Weals she has carried ever since.* Dr. Jessopp in his *Coming of the Friars* (art. " Black Death "), and Thorold Rogers in *Work and Wages*, deal with the permanent effects of the Black Death upon the peasantry. See herein ll. 286 *sqq.*

IV. l. 273. *Pied :* the Dominican friars were sometimes so called, whose habit was black-and-white.

IV. l. 388. *Winking Rood :* at Boxley, in Kent.

BOOK V. line 4. *His minion :* Alice Perrers.

V. l. 36. *The Miller, John Ball.* Of these and other heroes of the Peasants' Revolt the best account by far is that of G. M. Trevelyan in *England in the Age of Wycliffe*, with its accompanying

NOTES

volume of *Documents*. There are others, one, notably, by Professor Oman ; but Mr. Trevelyan's is the best.

V. l. 123. *Souse :* bacon salted and soaked.

V. l. 137. *Goliardise :* gluttony and revelling of sorts. As to the *goliardi*, sung by Walter Map in the well-known *Mihi est propositum*, the reader will find a good account in Wright's edition of the poet, done for the Camden Society.

V. l. 165. *John Schep :* another hero of the Revolt.

V. l. 178. *Piepowder.* The Court of *Pied-poudré* was one of summary jurisdiction held by charter within the market or fair for offences committed against the peace, or the market franchise.

V. l. 181. *Canterbury.* Archbishop Sudbury was particularly obnoxious to the Rebels. As Chancellor he was held responsible for the Poll Tax, as Archbishop he had imprisoned John Ball. He was a friend, also, of John of Gaunt. All these things were heavily against him.

V. ll. 184, 185, 187. *Weyhill, St. Frideswide, St. Giles :* famous fairs, all three of them. It was at fairs and markets that news between county and county mainly passed.

V. l. 226. *Bampton, Commissioner :* see his deeds in Trevelyan, *op. cit.* pp. 207–8.

V. l. 230. *Trailbaston.* There is a vast amount of lore connected with the Commission and Court of Trailbaston, fairly collected by old Cowell in his *Interpreter* under the heading " Justices of Trailbaston." It was an extraordinary and summary jurisdiction, founded by Edward I., a sort of irregular assize, which proceeded upon a special commission. The *baston* was no doubt a staff of office. " My lord " in the text was Sir John Cavendish, Chief Justice of the King's Bench. He was sent down into Essex to restore order, armed with his commission (Trevelyan, pp. 208 *sqq.*).

V. l. 256. *The Wearer of the Ring :* Sudbury, Archbishop of Canterbury.

V. l. 304. *John the Miller.* See this song, which I have tinkered a little, in Trevelyan.

V. l. 330. *Legge.* John Legge was collector of the Poll Tax. Read of him in Trevelyan.

V. l. 334. *Hales.* Robert Hales was Treasurer.

NOTES

Book VI. line 55. *Holland . . . Warwick . . . Tiptoft . . . Suffolk*. Holland was Henry Duke of Exeter ; Warwick was Nevill the Kingmaker ; Tiptoft was Earl of Worcester, the first italianate Englishman on record ; Suffolk was Delapole, the Jack Nape of popular execration. The text-books deal fairly by them all ; the best, I think, is Sir James Ramsay's *Lancaster and York*.

VI. l. 57. *Merchant of his age :* Edward IV., a great woolmonger.

VI. l. 65. *The fat and smooth and white :* The adjectives are Sir Thomas More's, in his *Life of King Edward the Fifth*, a beautiful tract.

VI. l. 85. *Jack Mend-all :* Jack Cade, treated too lightly by all historians except Sir James Ramsay in *Lancaster and York*.

VI. l. 99. *The long-legg'd king :* Edward I., virtual founder of Parliament as we know it.

VI. l. 142. *While Nene ran full :* the battle of Northampton, July 10, 1460.

VI. l. 161. *The Devil's Water :* the battle of Hexham, May 15, 1464. The Devil's Water is a stream, on the banks of which, in a meadow called The Linnels, the battle was fought.

VI. l. 163. *René's haggard daughter :* Margaret of Anjou.

VI. l. 167. *Another Spring ;* the battle of Barnet, April 14, 1471.

VI. l. 176. *The Black Snake of Anjou :* Fulk of that family, fabled to be the fruit of devil's intercourse.

Book VII. line 33. *Radmore Plain.* The battle of Bosworth was fought out here, a good way south of Market Bosworth, on August 22, 1485.

VII. l. 46. *Little of Gaunt.* Henry VII.'s title to the throne, such as it was, depended upon the legitimization of John of Gaunt's children by Catherine Swynford, and even so was a female descent. He bettered it by marrying Edward IV.'s daughter Elizabeth. As Professor Pollard points out (*Reign of Henry VII.*, I. xvii.), the marriage was "as essential to his position as was William III.'s with Mary II. to his."

VII. l. 57. *Others' lust.* It is sufficient to mention the still rank-smelling names of Empson and Dudley.

VII. l. 92. *Champion land :* open land, held by the tenants in common and shifting ownership. The word is common in Tusser.

232

NOTES

VII. l. 133.   *Gresham and Paget . . . :* names, taken as they come, of great families which had their rise in the wreck of feudalism. The Wars of the Roses destroyed the Norman aristocracy, but the new men out-Normanned it.   The end of the hard-held privileges of tenants " by the custom of the manor " and the beginning of the despot-landlords of the 18th and 19th centuries coincide.

VII. l. 138.   *Grosvenor* is rich : an allusion to the old Scrope and Grosvenor controversy of the 14th century, when Grosvenor was a respectable name, but no more.   In this century he gained the *garb* in more senses than one.

VII. l. 200.   *And pack a Parliament:* " The Parliament which met on November 3, 1529, was destined to carry out a series of changes more profound and wide-reaching than any which had yet been accomplished in the annals of English legislation.   In the seven years of its existence it snapped the bonds which bound England to Rome, and established the royal supremacy over the English Church" (*Political History of England*, V. 291). As to " packing," " A letter from Gardiner to Wolsey proves that Henry was interested in the choice of candidates for the shires of Nottingham and Derby, Bedford and Buckingham, and the town of Southampton.   The King wrote with his own hand to the borough of Colchester, requesting the corporation to return a candidate whom he had nominated ; and Richard Hall, the biographer of Bishop Fisher, states that every writ was accompanied by a private letter from one or other of the King's Council, directing the choice of the electors.   That the majority of the House consisted of Crown officials is admitted by the most protestant of contemporary chroniclers" (*ibid.*).

VII. l. 15.   *Two crosses:* that of York, and that of Cardinal-Legate.

VII. l. 244.   *For when you put your broad lands out.* The practice of farming out the lands of the monasteries was general at the time of the Dissolution, and in every way disastrous.

VII. l. 256.   *Away with Gracedieu:* The Cistercians in particular had beautiful names for their convents.

VII. l. 285.   *That they anon could sack the King.* This is where the whirligig of time brought one of his revenges.   Out of the spoils of the monasteries the Crown raised up a new class of

NOTES

landlords, the squires as we know them. That class it was
which in 1649 brought down the Crown.

VII. l. 293. *His Polar Star* : Niccolo Macchiavelli, the Florentine,
whose handbook of despotry, *The Prince*, was, and still is, fatal
reading for politicians.

VII. l. 304. *Struck sideways at the Virgin-Mother* : when he spoiled
the shrines and broke up the images. It may have been
forced upon him by the logic of events ; it may have pleased
the Genevan faction ; it may have been judged necessary to
salvation. But it is a hard matter to secure your own salvation
at the cost of a people's gods. So far as may be I have satisfied
myself that the English peasantry went without a working
religion for two hundred years—that is, from the time when
King and Parliament had obliterated Catholicism to tle time
of John Wesley.

VII. l. 310. *Curch :* a woman's head-dress.

VII. l. 317. *One was gaunt :* Mary.

VII. l. 321. *And left dry sticks, for fools to plant.* Elizabeth was the
complete despot, *fruges consumere nata*. What she left over were
the sapless rudiments of despotry, from which the Stuarts reaped
their barren harvest.

VII. l. 330. *He laid hands on the coin in mint.* Henry's debasing of
the coinage was his last robbery, unless the suppression of the
Guilds can be scored against him. See Thorold Roges (*Work
and Wages*) upon the coinage question.

VII. l. 335. *The badge : Fidei Defensor.*

VII. l. 338. *Nay, if like man the Master is* . . . The conclusion of
this and the following line is involved in the renunciation of
his faith. He claimed to be God's anointed, but if he rejected
the God by whom he was anointed the anointing would go
with the rejection. The reasoning was popular if unsound.
It was sound enough, at any rate, to settle the Stuart pretensions.

VII. l. 342. *The Estate :* the Commons' estate, as England knew it
until the Reform Bill.

VII. i. 363. *Triple mail : robur et aes triplex.*

VII. l. 380. *When Justices o' the Peace* . . . This is one of the
landmarks of the peasants' oppression. Here is Hsbach's
account of it : " The Act of 1562 . . . provides that any

234

person between the ages of ten and eighteen may become an apprentice in husbandry, and when so bound must serve till the age of twenty-one or twenty-four. The wages of servants and day-labourers are to be assessed by the Justices of the Peace, with the assistance of the Sheriff, 'if he conveniently may'; and it is made punishable either to give or to take higher wages. No labourer is to leave the place of his abode without a certificate from the authorities, which he must show whenever he attempts to obtain work" (Hasbach, *The English Agricultural Labourer*, p. 41). When it is remembered that Justices were inevitably landlords, the bearing of the Act becomes plain enough.

VII. l. 419. *His weed and root :* his tobacco and potato.

VII. l. 451. *Court Halimote :* the old manorial court, not yet dead.

BOOK VIII. line 51. *The men whose need is to possess you . . .* The landed class. A true saying from Hasbach (*op. cit.* p. 71): "It is among the deepest convictions of the English middle-classes that the 16th-century struggle for the purity of religion and the 17th-century struggle for personal liberty are among the greatest achievements of the nation. It is remarkable that the lower classes should also have accepted this conviction. The Reformation robbed them of the institutions which had helped them in their times of need, and parliamentary government produced a class domination which took their land from them, threw on them a great part of the burdens entailed by trade wars and colonial wars, and pitilessly abandoned them to the storm which broke over them with the rise of the great industry." That is so true that comment is unnecessary, even such a comment as that the whole of this Poem is itself a comment upon it.

VIII. l. 67. *Who sought to quicken the dead with air :* James II., whose efforts to re-establish the Catholic Church were of that absurd futility.

VIII. l. 110. *When the Commons locked the door . . .* March 2, 1629, was the date of this significant act. It was the first stroke of Civil War, first stroke at Charles's head too.

VIII. l. 115. *They made that true, not truly spoken.* The words were Eliot's, and were not true at the time. The Civil War made

NOTES

them true, and so they have finally remained, in spite of George III., who broke some Parliaments without being broken up himself.

VIII. 1. 133. *He was estranged.* Nothing is more remarkable than the obliteration of the peasant in this time of anarchy. The best account known to me of the state of the countryside during the Civil War—and even there it is implied rather than expressed—is in the Verney Memoirs, of which there are four volumes in print. I wish there were four dozen—as I believe there might be.

VIII. 1. 159. *Dom Galfrid :* a hint at the old days, in the memorial brass of a bygone rector.

VIII. 1. 184. *In England now surg'd up a force :* I mean the Middle Class, sown in the towns, and now emerging as the power in the state which was to become the predominant power in 1832. The Middle Class, as I understand the matter, was not perfectly autochthonous, nor wholly super-imposed. It had been gathered from all over Europe, and was very much a residuum. Having, no doubt, an English base, there drifted into it in succession settling Norsemen, imported Normans, then Flemings and Walloons, then Genoese (called Lombards in the fourteenth century), and a liberal sprinkling of Jews, until their expulsion. A history of the Middle Class has yet to be written, to show both its service and its disservice of the state. During the two and a half centuries still before us, that class represented by such bodies as the Freemen of Westminster and the London burgesses, was the very buttress of Liberty. The Reform Act made most of them Conservatives, and the rest academic Liberals of the Bright and Cobden type. They have been our masters ever since.

VIII. 1. 248. *The Medicean effigy :* Charles II., who had this blood from his mother. His portraits are startlingly like those of Lorenzo the Magnificent.

VIII. 1. 256. *Now we get hire and whores from France.* . . . By the secret treaty of Dover, in 1670, Charles was to declare himself a Catholic as soon as he conveniently might. " To repress possible disorder among turbulent and unquiet subjects, Louis was to aid his ally with 2,000,000 *livres* and 6000 soldiers "

236

NOTES

(*Political History of England*, VIII., 101). Louis de Quérouaille was Louis' decoy-duck ; but the principal French agent for the treaty was Charles's own sister, the Duchess of Orleans.

VIII. 1. 262. *Bagwell's wife.* . . . Bagwell was a shipwright of Deptford, and his wife one of Pepys's many light loves. Plenty of her in the Diary.

VIII. 1. 292. *Tied him securely to the land :* by the Act 13 & 14, Car. II., c. 12. Under this Act labourers were practically confined to their parishes, since it provided that " any newcomer, within forty days of arrival, could be ejected from a parish by an order from the magistrates, upon complaint from the parish officer, and removed to the parish where he or she was last legally settled." This was tantamount to a reduction of the peasantry to the old condition of villeinage, since the only provisions for exemption contained in the Act were (*a*) that the stranger should have settled in a tenement of £10 yearly value, or (*b*) could give security for the discharge of the parish to the magistrate's satisfaction (Hammond, *The Village Labourer*, pp. 112 *sqq.*). The preamble to this reactionary decree declares its object to be the prevention of vagabondage. The real object, however, depended upon a statute of 43 Elizabeth, which made each parish responsible for the poor within it.

VIII. 1. 295. *The village till was answerable :* by Statute 43 Elizabeth referred to in the preceding note.

BOOK IX. line 58. Μηδὲν ἄγαν. " It hath been the wisdom of the Church of *England*, ever since the first compiling of her Publick Liturgy, to keep the mean between the two extremes, of too much stiffness in refusing, and of too much easiness in admitting, any variation from it."

IX. 1. 73. *When George Fox* . . . This is his widow's account of the beginning of his ministry.

IX. 1. 103. *And the Gray Men from oversea :* The Franciscans, between whose ministry and that of Wesley and his Preachers the analogies are remarkable. See the book hereof called *Bonaccord*.

IX. 1. 118. *That Pentecostal Eve :* May 24, 1738.

IX. 1. 139. *Says he* . . . These are the famous Five Points which mark a Methodist.

237

NOTES

IX. 1. 156. *So Hoage, with Christ-love all astir.* . . . There is a
fine account of the effects of Methodism upon a peasant in
Lackington's *Memoirs.* Although Lackington wrote his book
after he had become a prosperous tradesman, and scornful of
Methodism, he was unable to keep out some of the glow of
enthusiasm which his conversion wrought in him. He convinces
his reader in spite of himself.

IX. 1. 176. *The sot in ermine :* George I.

BOOK X. line 82. *Champion-land.* See note to VII. 92.

X. 1. 85. *Keep watchful eye for grassy ridges.* . . . They can be seen
all over England to this day. There have been several good
general accounts of the Common Field system of husbandry
since Seebohm's, to which I have referred already, although
that remains, I think, the best. But a very good particular
account of it, from which the general practice can be gathered,
is in Mr. Warde Fowler's *Kingham, Old and New* (Blackwell,
1913). Kingham is manor in Oxfordshire.

X. 1. 94. *The village lay, a little realm* . . . This state of affairs,
without reactionism or archaicism, is the thing to aim at if the
peasant is ever to become a responsible person. Enlarge the
powers of the Parish Councils, restrict those of the County
Councils to county affairs. Give the parishes power to levy
a rate. Have no fear. There is no more cautious, and no
more democratic, body in the country than a Parish Council ;
for nowhere else are the people's representatives so closely in
touch with the electorate.

X. 1. 170. *The plan found good* . . . For a savage, but not at all
too savage, account of the working of Enclosure Acts consult
Hammond, *The Village Labourer.* Hasbach, *The English Agricultural Labourer,* is to the same effect ; but he is very dull
reading.

X. 1. 214. *His Grace the Duke* . . . Here is a short list of parks,
with their acreages : Arundel, 1216 acres ; Hatfield, with
Millwards, 1389 acres ; Clumber, 3776 acres ; Welbeck, with
woods, 4224 acres ; Longleat, with woods, 3777 acres ; Stowe,
1400 acres ; Wentworth Woodhouse, 1600 acres ; Woburn,
2310 acres ; Chatsworth, 2368 acres.

238

NOTES

X. l. 266. *Speenhamland* . . . a parish in Berkshire, now part of Newbury, where on May 6, 1795, the Berkshire magistrates met and " there resolved on a momentous policy which was gradually adopted in almost every part of England " (Hammond, *op. cit.* 161). The policy, which was charitably meant, was for the relief of the poor, and recommended that labourers' wages should be in proportion to the current price of corn ; the principle being that every man must have the equivalent of three gallon loaves of bread a week, his wife and each child one and a half. The effect of this disastrous proposal was, within a very few years, to pauperize the whole of the English peasantry already robbed of all their holding in the land. The subject is freely treated in Hammond and Hasbach (*op. cit.*).

X. l. 295. *For where else in the world d'you find* . . . The only answer is that of the text : Nowhere.

Book XI. line 6. *Where the Zadorra* : the river on whose plain was fought the decisive battle of Vittoria, June 21, 1813.

XI. l. 26. *A gibbet-shape* : at Winchester Assizes, when the rick-burners were tried and condemned in 1830.

XI. l. 80. *Which grip'd the Robber's heart in ice* : Moscow to the Beresina.

XI. l. 95. *And they stood firm* : at Waterloo.

XI. l. 112. *The Doctor* : Lord Sidmouth.

XI. l. 122. *A rogue* . . . : George IV., if ever there was one. Of this supreme rip it is instructive to remark what Christopher North thought fit to print in Blackwood in 1827 : " *North.* For his Majesty King George the Fourth, James, would I lay down my life. A better—a nobler king—never sat on the British throne. *Shepherd.* Deevil the ane." (*Noct. Ambros.* I. 382.)

XI. l. 131. *The Beau, the Poodle* . . . Beau Brummel, Poodle Byng.

XI. l. 133. *Holland House* : this, Bowood, and Woburn were all Whig houses.

XI. l. 151. *By hanging stragglers.* In 1810 Romilly introduced and carried a Bill in the House of Commons, abolishing the death penalty for the crimes of stealing privately to the amount of five shillings in a shop. It was rejected by the House of Lords,

NOTES

by a majority which included the Archbishop of Canterbury and six bishops. It was again rejected in 1813, five bishops in the majority. (*Hammond*, p. 204.)

XI. l. 167. *The passing of the Age of Bronze*: in his poem of that name, his last.

XI. l. 179. *Speenhamlond: supra*, X. 266. As to the rick-burnings, one of the best accounts is in *Hammond*. For the working of the Speenhamland proposals in 1822 let the reader consult Cobbett's *Political Register* for September of that year, where the Hampshire scale of allowances for the poor are set out at length. As Cobbett says in comment, such treatment was not "tying up one hand" but "sewing up the mouth."

XI. l. 204. *The Reverend Mr. Hare* . . . This is Augustus Hare, a gentle prig, of whose troubles in Wilts during the rick-burnings we may read in *Memorials of a Quiet Life*.

XI. l. 217. *Down goes his Grace* . . . The Duke of Wellington, as Lord Lieutenant of Hampshire, sat on the Bench during the Bloody Assize at Winchester. "When the special commission had finished its labours at Winchester, 101 peasants had been capitally convicted : of these six were left for execution. The remaining 95 were, with few exceptions, transported for life. . . . Not a single life had been taken by the rioters, not a single person wounded" (*Hammond*, p. 288). In the event there was such an outcry that only two were hanged at Winton ; but all the prisoners were compelled to witness the executions.

XI. l. 239. *Who sees our Three Estates so just* . . . "I have never read or heard of any measure up to the present moment which can in any degree satisfy my mind that the state of the representation can be improved, or rendered more satisfactory than at the present moment. I am fully convinced that the country already possesses a legislature which answers all the purposes of good legislation " . . . (The Duke's *Speech on Reform*, Nov. 2, 1830).

XI. l. 256. *Foul spawn of that self-lover* . . . The self-lover was Charles I., his spawn was Charles II., foul enough ; in whose reign it was that most of the rotten boroughs, Cornish group and what-not, were created.

240

NOTES

XI. l. 262.   *Together workt to one end—Rent!*
  " Safe in their barns, these Sabine tillers sent
    Their brethren out to battle.   Why ?   For rent ! "
                                   The Age of Bronze, XIV. 618.

XI. l. 312.   *A turn of wheat bread for his meal* . . .: when Peel broke down the Corn Law.

XI. l. 317.   *While rise the Union's iron walls:* The first work of the reformed Parliament was to break the old Poor Law.   Outdoor relief, as established by the Speenhamland decree, was abolished, and with it went the attendant evils of pauperizing and sweating the poor in favour of the ratepayers.   But to abolish outdoor relief and put nothing in its place but the workhouse was certainly a " comment grim."

Book XII. line 72.   *He had the House instead of the Dole :* see preceding note.

XII. l. 89.   *The house is tied :* when the cottage is tied to the farm and the tenant's occupancy is reckoned a part of his wages.   Then the rule is, Out of work out of doors.

XII. l. 94.   *Now is the hour of rail and steam.*   I have put a middle date to this momentous hour.   Railway operations began on an extended scale about 1836 and continued till 1844, when there was a sharp decline.

XII. l. 133.   *There mote he learn* . . .   I use the optative to indicate that he might have learned the discipline of the Trades Union, though in fact he never did.

XII. l. 135.   *While Honour has her bosomful.* . . .   There is much that is shameful sticking to the name of Trade Union—pressure upon non-union men and the like.   But the most shameful thing of all is that the whole weight of the association is turned to the protection of bad, slow and idle workmen.

XII. l. 221.   *That should he catch the Whigs a-bathing :* when he " dished " them with his Reform Bill of 1867.

XII. l. 257.   *And peasants dwindle* . . .   Some tables from the Board of Agriculture in my possession show that in 1851 the number of " persons employed in agriculture in England and Wales " was 1,513,778 ; in 1901, 921,424.

XII. l. 262.   *Alas ! good Queen* . . .   " She announced the

NOTES

Exhibition [of 1851] as the greatest triumph of Peace which the world had ever seen " (Martin, *Prince Consort*, II. 405, cited in *Political History*, XII. 92 *n*.).

XII. l. 299. *He:* The German Emperor, symbolizing, as his business is, his countrymen's original blunder.

XII. I. 307. *Hodge and Hodge's lord . . .* I have put the covering dates of these conclusive Acts in the margin : 1872 was the Ballot Act ; 1883 the Franchise Act which made Hodge a citizen. This last work of justice and honour was, I believe, W. E. Forster's doing, not W. E. Gladstone's.

XII. l. 329. *To grant land-holding by an Act . . .* This is quite true. In 1906, when the Small Holdings cry ruled the election, the administration of it was given over to the County Councils, a squirearchy. In a county known to me a great man, a forty-thousand acre man, was chosen on the County Council—and afterwards had two compulsory sales forced upon him under the Small Holdings Act. His agent was responsible, no doubt ; but it was done under his nose.

XII. l. 334. *The village-mote's desire:* oblique reference to the Parish Council, which by the law of its being can only operate through the Rural District Council (farmers and small tradesmen) or the County Council (squires).

XII. l. 384. *Thanks to the length of Forster's arm:* W. E. Forster again, who drove the Education Act through, 1870–1.

XII. l. 385. *Out then, ye Dungflies . . .* see Book VI. for the foreshadowing of this infernal scourge of our times, made inevitable by the copulation of original sin and the Printing Press.

XII. l. 442. *Face you the Angel with the brand:* Justice.

XII. l. 446. *Escheat . . . :* that is escheat which falls back to the lord by forfeiture or default of heir.

Envoy, line 19. *You faced the dawn:* when he received the Franchise in 1883. By 1913 the first faint glimmerings of sunrise were discernible. Mr. Lloyd George's bid for the agricultural vote in the autumn of that year was one sign.

Id. l. 26. *Where first you saw him :* in the Prelude to this work.

Id. l. 60. *The mighty have opprest the weak . . .* Here, dramatically, is the *causa belli* as far as our people, apart from their

NOTES

governors, are concerned. They knew little of German pretensions, nothing of Austrian entanglements, nor did they fear, nor do they believe in, foreign hostile invasion. The attack on Belgian liberty moved them as they have never been moved before, and the knowledge gained afterwards of German bestial frenzy only intensified their purpose. For freedom they have always been willing to fight, and for it have been fighting their masters for a thousand years. But this is the first time that, as a race, they have risen, practically *en masse*, for the Idea of Freedom, as it has revealed itself in the noble Belgian nation, its protomartyr.

Id. l. 115. *The bar of Spain* . . . : the Pyrenees, where the Saracen invasion was arrested.

Id. l. 179. *The forest on the ridge :* Savernake.

Id. l. 212. *Sarum :* Old Sarum, where it is probable that the old Domesday was proclaimed. See note to I. 226.

Id. l. 421. *As I decree* . . . Some national resumption of land—if land be not offered spontaneously—must be made if the State will heed the call of honour as sharply as the Peasantry heeded that of human necessity. I have not the figures, though they should be known, but on a cautious estimate it seems that twenty per cent. of " persons engaged in agriculture," who are of all ages, both sexes, and varying degrees of qualification, volunteered for active service : an astounding thing.* Even more astounding is it that they should have heard and understood the call. I hope, though not without qualms of doubt, that some great act of national gratitude will be rendered to the working-classes of Great Britain, to crown the worthiest international part Great Britain has ever played.

* In round numbers, 250,000 peasants have volunteered.

PRINTED IN GREAT BRITAIN BY
RICHARD CLAY & SONS, LIMITED,
BRUNSWICK ST., STAMFORD ST., S.E.,
AND BUNGAY, SUFFOLK.